DK POCKET EYEWITNESS

DOGS

FACTS AT YOUR FINGERTIPS

DK DELHI
Senior editor Neha Gupta
Editor Ishani Nandi
Art editors Nidhi Mehra, Shipra Jain, Nishesh Batnagar
Jacket designer Juhi Sheth
Jackets editorial coordinator Priyanka Sharma
DTP designers Jagtar Singh, Jaypal Singh Chauhan
Picture researcher Sumedha Chopra
Managing editor Alka Thakur Hazarika
Managing art editor Romi Chakraborty
CTS manager Balwant Singh
Production manager Pankaj Sharma

DK LONDON
Senior editor Caroline Stamps
Senior art editor Rachael Grady
Managing editor Gareth Jones
Managing art editor Philip Letsu
Jacket designer Surabhi Wadhwa-Gandhi
Jacket editor Amelia Collins
Jacket design development manager Sophia MTT
Producer (pre-production) Rebecca Fallowfield
Producer (print production) Vivienne Yong

Publisher Andrew Macintyre
Associate publishing director Liz Wheeler
Art director Phil Ormerod
Publishing director Jonathan Metcalf

Consultant Dr Kim Dennis-Bryan

This edition published in 2018
First published in Great Britain in 2014
by Dorling Kindersley Limited
80 Strand, London WC2R 0RL

Copyright © 2014, 2018 Dorling Kindersley Limited
A Penguin Random House Company
10 9 8 7 6 5 4 3 2 1
001–310511–Oct/18

A CIP catalogue record for this book
is available from the British Library.

ISBN: 978-0-2413-4360-9

Printed and bound in China

A WORLD OF IDEAS:
SEE ALL THERE IS TO KNOW

www.dk.com

CONTENTS

Chihuahua

Breed recognition
The breeds in this book are
recognized by official societies
such as the UK Kennel Club,
the American Kennel Club,
or the Fédération Cynologique
Internationale (FCI).

Scales and sizes
This book contains
scale drawings of dogs
to show how tall they
are with relation to
an average adult male.
The measurement is
taken from a dog's feet
to the top of its neck.

1.8 m
(6 ft)

The dog

Domestic dogs are descended from the Grey Wolf. At least 14,000 years ago, some wolves began to wander into human villages looking for food. People realized that the friendliest of these animals could be tamed and trained to help them with various tasks, such as hunting and guarding.

Skeleton

Dogs are designed to hunt. They have a flexible skeleton that allows them to run quickly. The position of the eye sockets towards the sides of the skull makes dogs excellent at judging distance.

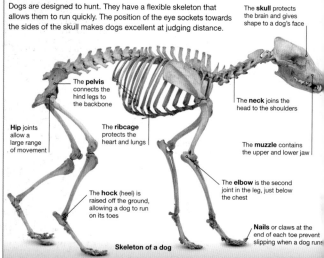

The **skull** protects the brain and gives shape to a dog's face

The **pelvis** connects the hind legs to the backbone

The **neck** joins the head to the shoulders

Hip joints allow a large range of movement

The **ribcage** protects the heart and lungs

The **muzzle** contains the upper and lower jaw

The **hock** (heel) is raised off the ground, allowing a dog to run on its toes

The **elbow** is the second joint in the leg, just below the chest

Nails or claws at the end of each toe prevent slipping when a dog runs

Skeleton of a dog

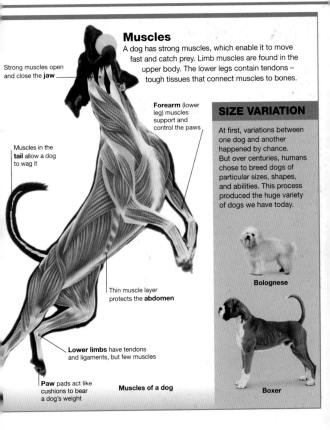

Muscles

A dog has strong muscles, which enable it to move fast and catch prey. Limb muscles are found in the upper body. The lower legs contain tendons – tough tissues that connect muscles to bones.

Strong muscles open and close the **jaw**

Forearm (lower leg) muscles support and control the paws

Muscles in the **tail** allow a dog to wag it

Thin muscle layer protects the **abdomen**

Lower limbs have tendons and ligaments, but few muscles

Paw pads act like cushions to bear a dog's weight

Muscles of a dog

SIZE VARIATION

At first, variations between one dog and another happened by chance. But over centuries, humans chose to breed dogs of particular sizes, shapes, and abilities. This process produced the huge variety of dogs we have today.

Bolognese

Boxer

The dog family

Animals that belong to the dog family, or Canidae, are called canids. All wild canids hunt or scavenge for food, which they usually find with their noses. Altogether, there are 35 dog species – here are six of the most widely distributed canids.

CANIDAE

GREY WOLF

Domestic dogs are descended from the Grey Wolf.

GOLDEN JACKAL

Jackals live in dry, open spaces. Golden, or Common, Jackals are the most widespread, being found in both Asia and Africa.

AFRICAN HUNTING DOG

African Hunting Dogs have a patchy coat with areas of red, black, brown, white, and yellow fur. These endangered creatures hunt in packs, just like wolves.

Wolves live and hunt in packs. Grey Wolves are the most common, and are found mainly in Canada, Alaska, and Asia, but there are also some in Europe.

WHERE DID DOGS COME FROM?

The earliest member of the Canidae probably lived about 40 million years ago. It had slightly longer legs than its tree-dwelling ancestors and spent more time on the ground hunting prey. It had sharp teeth and acute hearing – characteristics also found in canids today.

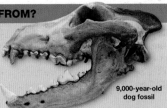

9,000-year-old dog fossil

MANED WOLF

Native to South America, **Maned Wolves** have incredibly long legs, so they can hunt in tall grass.

RED FOX

Foxes are characterized by their pointed ears and snout, and long, bushy tail. They live in small family groups. The **Red Fox** can be found in most parts of the world.

RACCOON DOG

Raccoon Dogs live in Europe and Asia. They are good climbers (unusual for a canid) as well as expert swimmers. They eat frogs and fish.

Heads and ears

Since humans first tamed the Grey Wolf, they have changed
its appearance dramatically through selective breeding, and so
modern dogs have a range of different features. Both
the shape of a dog's head and its ear type vary
greatly across different breeds.

Heads

A dog's head is defined by the length of its
muzzle – short, medium, or long. Muzzle
length affects a dog's ability to follow
a scent – generally, the longer it is,
the better a dog's sense of smell.

Short muzzle
(Bulldog)

Medium muzzle
(German Pointer)

Long muzzle
(Saluki)

Ears

There are three main ear shapes for a dog: erect (standing up), semi-erect (half standing up), and drop (hanging down). The shape of a dog's ears is specific to each breed.

Drop
(Beagle)

Erect
(Alaskan Malamute)

Erect: Candle-Flame
(English Toy Terrier)

Semi-erect: Rose
(Greyhound)

Semi-erect: Button (Pug)

Drop: Pendant
(Bloodhound)

Coats and colours

Some dogs have short hair, some have long hair, some have silky hair, some have wiry hair... and some have almost no hair! In a few breeds (such as this Komondor below), long hair forms cords that look a bit like dreadlocks.

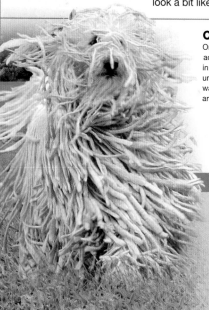

Coat types

Originally, dogs' coats were adapted to suit their lives – in cold climates, for example, undercoats would be thick and warm. Today, many unusual coat are decorative rather than useful.

Corded
(Komondor)

COLOUR VARIETIES

Dogs have coats in lots of colours and patterns. Some dog have markings on their bodies. Some colour types have unique names, such as "harlequin," for a black-and-white Great Dane.

White, cream, or grey

Gold or fawn

Wire-haired
(Giant Schnauzer)

**Full
double**
(Chow Chow)

Short
(Dalmatian)

Long straight
(Maltese)

Curly
(Labradoodle)

Hairless
(Mexican Hairless)

Liver
or red

Blue

Dark brown
or chocolate

Black

Gold, tan, or
liver and white

Black
and white

Black, tan,
and white

Liver
and tan

Blue
and tan

Black
and tan

Brindle

Variety of
colours

Senses

Dogs have the same senses as we do – hearing, smell, sight, taste, and touch – but they use them in ways different to us. The senses we use most are not the most important ones for dogs.

Sight

Dogs don't see red or green: their world is yellow, blue, and grey. Their sight isn't as good as ours in full light, but it's sharper in dim light, which is especially useful when hunting for food at dawn or dusk.

Smell and taste

Dogs have fewer taste buds than us. For them, smell is more important than taste – they use it to track prey, find their way, and locate other creatures. A dog's sense of smell is much better than ours.

Hearing

Dogs can move each ear separately to pick up signals from several directions. Their hearing abilities are sharp enough to hear sounds from four times farther away than our hearing allows. They can also hear high-pitched sounds that people can't detect.

Chihuahua

Touch

Like human babies, puppies love to cuddle up to their mum. They also play with other puppies to learn how to make friends, and how to fight. Whiskers help dogs to detect things that they can't see clearly.

Behaviour

Dogs are a lot like people in terms of their needs. Being pack animals, they are social in nature and get attached to animals and humans around them. They can show excitement, nervousness, and fear, all of which can be seen in the way they behave.

Body language

When dogs are calm, they relax their tail and ears. When happy, they wag their tail and when anxious, they raise it. Confiden dogs stand tall, but when frightened or shy, they crouch towards the ground.

Showing belly – a sig of submission

COMMUNICATION

Most dogs bark when they fight, play, or are excited. Sometimes they do so as a warning or to attract attention.

Dogs howl when they are alone, as a way of looking for company. They have taken this habit from their ancestors – wolves.

Dogs tend to whine when they are sad or lonely, or when they feel afraid or excited.

Territorial Instinct

Whether they live in packs or families, dogs protect their territory and react when they see, hear, or smell anything they don't recognize. They raise the alarm when they see strangers around them.

A German Shepherd barks to protect its space

Dogs and people

When people first tamed wolves, they used them as hunters and guards. Modern dogs still do these jobs and more too – they can be herders, guides, and trackers, and they can even help blind and sick people.

Going hunting with Foxhounds

Hunting

In the past, people used dogs to help them hunt for food. Today, they also help people hunt for sport. Dogs are ideally suited to hunting as they are predators. They are fast and intelligent, and have an excellent sense of smell.

Transport

Before there were cars and trucks, dogs were sometimes used to pull carts. Dogs were especially useful in mountainous areas not suitable for vehicles. In some icy regions, dog sleds are still used as a means of travel.

A Bernese Mountain Dog pulling a cart

Border Collie participating in an agility competition

Sports

Apart from their role in hunting, dogs also participate in other sporting events, such as agility competitions. On these occasions, dogs race through an obstacle course, jumping fences, weaving around poles, and dashing through tunnels.

OLD FRIENDS

A Nordic Bronze Age rock carving

Discovered in an ancient cave in Sweden, this carving tells the story of humans working with their canine companions. Similar carvings have been found all over the world.

Breed groups

Dogs are divided into groups (such as terriers), and then into breeds (such as the Boston Terrier). Groups vary from place to place, so these are not scientific classifications.

Classification

An officially recognized breed has a standard that includes information such as colour, weight, and size. Popular breeds are found all over the world, while others are well-known only in their country of origin.

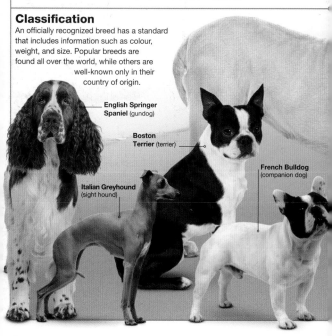

English Springer Spaniel (gundog)

Boston Terrier (terrier)

French Bulldog (companion dog)

Italian Greyhound (sight hound)

WHAT'S THAT DOG?

All dogs have the same scientific name – *Canis familiaris*. When people selectively bred dogs, they created the breeds we know today, such as the Pug (left). There are endless varieties of *Canis familiaris*.

Mastiff
(working dog)

Labradinger
(crossbreed)

Grand Basset Griffon Vendéen
(scent hound)

Siberian Husky
(spitz-type dog)

Dogs have most sweat glands on the

bottom of their paws

STAYING COOL
Dogs are high-energy animals, and constant activity causes their body temperatures to rise. Sweat released through glands under their paws and around their nose creates a cooling effect. A dog can also reduce its body heat by licking its nose to keep it moist and, most obviously, by panting.

Working dogs

The dogs in this group tend to be large and powerful, and include breeds traditionally developed for farm work such as herding and guarding. Nowadays, they are also used to protect homes or rescue people in danger. Therapy dogs are specially trained to help people with physical or emotional disabilities. Some schools have even started to use dogs for children to read aloud to, as it can help a reluctant reader gain confidence.

LIFELONG FRIENDS
Helen Keller, the famous American deaf-blind author and activist, loved dogs. She owned many breeds, including German Shepherds and Collies.

What is a working dog?

The group "working dogs" includes strong breeds that can perform tasks ranging from herding to guarding and combat. They vary in build: guard dogs are big and powerful, while sheep dogs are fast and light.

Herding

For centuries, dogs have helped farmers look after their livestock. Cattle dogs nip at the heels of the animals to keep them moving, while sheep dogs, such as the Collie (left), control a flock by circling them and responding to a shepherd's commands.

Taking care

Some working dog breeds also serve as therapy dogs. They provide comfort and affection to sick or disabled people. These dogs can also be trained to carry things for them and warn them of danger.

Search and rescue

When people get lost in the wilderness, or get buried during an earthquake or avalanche, rescuers use search dogs to find them. These dogs can follow a scent even in harsh conditions, while their strength and stamina can keep them going for a long time.

A German Shepherd
n a rescue operation

Guarding and fighting

People keep watchdogs to protect their homes, and the police use specially trained breeds to catch criminals. In war zones, dogs are used to detect mines (buried explosives), as well as for finding wounded soldiers.

Working dogs

For centuries, dogs have played many important roles in our lives. Herding livestock, guarding property, and helping with rescues are some of the countless jobs working dogs perform for us.

FOCUS ON...
JOBS FOR DOGS
Dogs can be trained to perform a wide variety of tasks.

Newfoundland

Believed to be of Canadian origin, this giant dog has a slightly oily, waterproof coat. Because it is a good swimmer, fishermen once used the powerful, water-loving Newfoundland to haul fishing nets out of the water. Today, it sometimes assists in sea rescues.

ORIGIN Canada

HEIGHT 66–71 cm (26–28 in)

COLOUR Brown; black

Thick fur protects against icy waters

Fila Brasileiro

Also known as the Brazilian Mastiff, this large working breed has excellent tracking abilities. Upon finding its prey, the Fila Brasileiro does not attack but stops it from escaping until told what to do. This ability, along with its strength, makes it a good police dog.

ORIGIN Brazil

HEIGHT 60–75 cm (24–30 in)

COLOUR Brindle; any solid colour

Sniffer dogs detect legal substances, such s drugs and explosives.

▲ Police dogs chase and hold suspects for questioning or arrest.

◀ Search-and-rescue dogs help to track down missing people.

Forelegs more heavily boned than hind legs

Dogo Argentino

This well-built dog was developed from 10 different canine types, including mastiffs, the Bulldog, and the Cordoba Fighting Dog (now extinct). Although it is a determined hunter, this breed has a gentle and loyal nature.

Strong muscles around neck

Broad, deep chest

ORIGIN Argentina

HEIGHT 60–68 cm (24–27 in)

COLOUR White

Pembroke Welsh Corgi

Smaller than most herding dogs, the
Pembroke Welsh Corgi uses its long,
low-set body to slip underneath large
farm animals, such as cattle, as they
move. It then keeps the livestock
moving by nipping at their hooves.

ORIGIN UK

HEIGHT 25–30 cm (10–12 in)

COLOUR Gold; fawn; red; black and tan

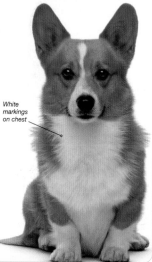

White
markings
on chest

Border Collie

This breed is known for its intelligence
and eagerness to learn. In 2011, a Border
Collie named Chaser gained worldwide fame for
being able to match more than 1,000 English
words to the correct objects.

ORIGIN UK

HEIGHT 50–53 cm
(20–21 in)

COLOUR
Variety of
colours

Bearded Collie

Once valued only as a sheepdog, this breed
is now also a popular pet. However, the Bearded
Collie requires wide, open spaces and is not
suited to a life in small homes.

ORIGIN UK

HEIGHT 51–56 cm
(20–22 in)

COLOUR Grey; fawn;
red-brown; blue; black

Old English Sheepdog

Farmers once docked (or shortened) the tails of these highly prized herding dogs to indicate their working status. This practice led to their other name – the Bobtail Sheepdog.

ORIGIN UK

HEIGHT 56–61 cm (22–24 in)

COLOUR Grey; blue

White markings on coat

Rough Collie

Attractive, intelligent, and loving, the Rough Collie was the perfect choice to play the title role in the classic *Lassie* films. Today, this breed is much admired as a pet and show dog.

ORIGIN UK

HEIGHT 51–61 cm (20–24 in)

COLOUR Gold; blue; gold and white; black, tan, and white

Shetland Sheepdog

With a long, beautiful coat, this breed bears a strong resemblance to the Rough Collie. Although it is smaller in size, the Shetland Sheepdog is an equally intelligent farm dog.

ORIGIN UK

HEIGHT 35–38 cm (14–15 in)

COLOUR Gold; blue; black and white; black and tan; black, tan, and white

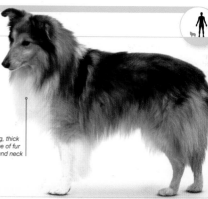

Long, thick mane of fur around neck

Mastiff

The large and powerful Mastiff is surprisingly calm and mild-mannered, considering it was once used for fighting in battles and dog-fights, as well as for bear- and bull-baiting.

ORIGIN UK

HEIGHT 70–77 cm (28–30 in)

COLOUR Fawn; brindle

Bulldog

A British symbol of determination and strength, the Bulldog has a distinctive look – a squat body, a tipped-back nose, and large flews (lips).

ORIGIN UK

HEIGHT 38–40 cm (15–16 in)

COLOUR Variety of colours

Thick, short forelegs set wide apart

Briard

In the past, the French mainly used the Briard to herd and protect livestock. Today, it makes a good watchdog because of its large size and protective instincts.

ORIGIN France

HEIGHT 58–69 cm (23–27 in)

COLOUR Grey; fawn; black

Also known as the Berger de Brie, the Briard is named after the French province of Brie.

Short, high-set, long-haired ears

Coat is long, flowing, and slightly wavy

Pyrenean Mountain Dog

This breed was also called the Pyrenean Wolfdog or Pyrenean Bearhound because it protected flocks from bears and wolves.

Used as a guardian for livestock in the French Pyrenees, this breed has powerful protective instincts. Because of its strength and endurance, it has also been used as a guard dog in wartime and as a sled puller.

ORIGIN	France
HEIGHT	65–70 cm (26–28 in)
COLOUR	White; white with tan patches

Tervueren

A popular working dog, the Tervueren has protective instincts that make it suitable for police work. Known for its quick mind and energy, this intelligent breed responds well to challenging tasks.

ORIGIN	Belgium
HEIGHT	56–66 cm (22–26 in)
COLOUR	Grey with black overlay; fawn with black overlay

Giant Schnauzer

The Giant Schnauzer was originally a farm dog. First recognized as obedient, intelligent, and easy to train during World War I, this breed is now often used as a guard and police dog.

ORIGIN	Germany
HEIGHT	60–70 cm (24–28 in)
COLOUR	Black; brindle

Rich, long coat

Dogue de Bordeaux

This mastiff-like breed is known for its broad head, short muzzle, and hanging jowls. Alert and protective, the Dogue de Bordeaux now lacks aggressive tendencies and makes a better companion than guard dog.

ORIGIN	France
HEIGHT	58–68 cm (23–27 in)
COLOUR	Fawn

Hanging jowls

German Shepherd Dog

Originally used for herding livestock, these brave dogs are nowadays used for rescue missions and police work. Many German Shepherds – the most famous being Rin Tin Tin – have also appeared in several popular films.

ORIGIN	Germany
HEIGHT	58–63 cm (23–25 in)
COLOUR	Gold; black; black with tan

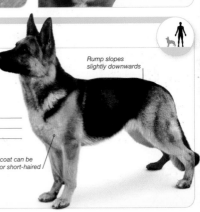

Rump slopes slightly downwards

Thick coat can be long- or short-haired

Great Dane

Bred for hunting large game in Germany, this gentle breed is best known for its gigantic build. Great Danes have often reached enormous physical sizes, but are slow to mature.

ORIGIN Germany

HEIGHT 71–76 cm (28–30 in)

COLOUR Fawn; blue; black; black and white; brindle

Broad muzzle

Black and white (harlequin) coat

In 2013, Zeus, a Great Dane, was identified as the world's tallest dog, measuring 1.15 m (3 ft 8 in) from paw to shoulder.

Hovawart

The Hovawart is a hardy breed that loves the outdoors, which makes it an ideal farm dog. It is believed that farmers used ancestors of the Hovawart in the 13th century.

ORIGIN Germany

HEIGHT 58–70 cm (23–28 in)

COLOUR Fawn; black; black and tan

Boxer

A mix of the English Bulldog and various mastiff-type breeds, this tall and powerful dog is affectionate, but also protective and intimidating when necessary. Bred for fighting, hunting, and farm work, the Boxer is today just as comfortable playing the role of a house dog.

ORIGIN	Germany
HEIGHT	53–63 cm (21–25 in)
COLOUR	Fawn; brindle

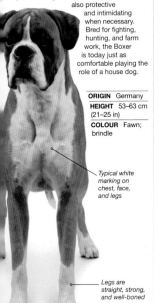

Typical white marking on chest, face, and legs

Legs are straight, strong, and well-boned

Neapolitan Mastiff

This giant dog breed is believed to be descended from Molossus war dogs that fought in Roman amphitheatres and during battles. Today, this breed is a choice for some police and armed forces.

ORIGIN	Italy
HEIGHT	60–75 cm (24–30 in)
COLOUR	Variety of colours

Short, grey coat

Rottweiler

Originally used as a cattle dog in southern Germany, the Rottweiler is a loyal and courageous dog that has a bad reputation it doesn't deserve. With the right training, this strongly protective breed can make a calm and loving pet.

ORIGIN	Germany
HEIGHT	58–69 cm (23–27 in)
COLOUR	Black and tan

A single search-and-rescue (SAR) dog can do the work of up to

30 human searchers

LIFESAVERS
Search-and-rescue dogs are specially trained to find people across a wide range of environments – in natural disasters such as earthquakes, through dense jungles, and even on mountain trails covered by ice and snow.

Bergamasco

Tough and powerfully built, the Bergamasco originated in the northern Italian mountains, where it was used as a sheepdog. This breed has a unique coat that is, at first, shaggy and long. As the dog grows, its hair forms dense mats known as "flocks". This type of coat protects the Bergamasco from the cold climate found at high altitudes.

Soft, long hair forms "flocks"

Oval-shaped feet with black nails

ORIGIN	Italy
HEIGHT	54–62 cm (21–24 in)
COLOUR	Grey; fawn; black

Dutch Schapendoes

Speed, strength, and agility are typical features of this breed. These qualities, along with its great stamina and high energy levels, make it a natural sheepdog.

ORIGIN	The Netherlands
HEIGHT	40–50 cm (16–20 in)
COLOUR	Any colour

Czechoslovakian Wolfdog

A cross between German Shepherds and grey wolves, the Czechoslovakian Wolfdog has inherited a number of traits from its wild ancestors. Although wary of strangers, this independent and fearless dog is faithful and obedient to people it knows.

ORIGIN	Czech Republic
HEIGHT	60–65 cm (24–26 in)
COLOUR	Grey

Mallorca Mastiff

Also known as the Ca de Bou, this powerful breed has a mastiff-type build. Once used for fighting and bull-baiting, the Mallorca Mastiff – though more friendly today than it once was – makes a better guard dog than a family pet.

ORIGIN	Spain
HEIGHT	52–58 cm (20–23 in)
COLOUR	Fawn; black; brindle

Distinctive lighter area on face

Portuguese Watchdog

The Portuguese Watchdog gets its other name, Rafeiro de Alentejo, from its place of origin. Big, strong, and protective, this working breed is used to guard property and livestock.

ORIGIN	Portugal
HEIGHT	64–74 cm (25–29 in)
COLOUR	Grey; fawn; black; brindle

Formidable in size and strength, the Portuguese Watchdog is the largest of the Portuguese dog breeds.

White markings on chest and legs

Pumi

Bred in the 18th century, the Pumi is a mixture of the Hungarian Puli and various terrier types. Inheriting the Puli's sharp hunting skills and a typical terrier's stamina, the Pumi makes a good herder and vermin-hunter.

ORIGIN	Hungary
HEIGHT	38–47 cm (15–19 in)
COLOUR	Cream; grey; gold; black

Narrow, terrierlike head

Well-muscled, lean body

Komondor

The Komondor is easily recognized by its white, corded, moplike hair. Despite its curious appearance, this is a strong-willed breed with great strength and intelligence, as well as good guarding and herding instincts.

Very long, heavy, corded coat

ORIGIN	Hungary
HEIGHT	60–80 cm (24–31 in)
COLOUR	White

Hungarian Puli

It is believed that nomadic tribes of Asia brought this energetic breed into Central Europe. Once used as a herding dog, the Hungarian Puli today makes an affectionate family pet.

ORIGIN	Hungary
HEIGHT	36–44 cm (14–17 in)
COLOUR	White; grey; fawn; black

Drop ears hidden
under coat

Komondors live with
the sheep they guard
and treat the flock as
pack members to
be protected.

Anatolian Shepherd Dog

Turkish shepherds once used this
powerful dog to protect their livestock
from large predators. Breeders made
the Anatolian Shepherd Dog similar
in size and colour to the livestock it
guarded so that it was less obvious
to potential attackers.

Mane of thicker hair
around shoulders

Fawn coat of
various shades

ORIGIN	Turkey
HEIGHT	71–81 cm (28–32 in)
COLOUR	Any colour

Bernese Mountain Dog

The Bernese Mountain Dog takes its name from the Swiss county Berne, where it was traditionally used to carry goods such as milk and cheese. Today, it is mainly kept as a pet, due to its friendly nature.

ORIGIN Switzerland

HEIGHT 58–70 cm (23–28 in)

COLOUR Black and tan with white markings

St Bernard

This breed is famous for rescuing travellers lost in the Alpine snow. Known as the Alpine Mastiff until 1880, it was given the name St Bernard after the monk who founded the place where this breed was first bred.

ORIGIN Switzerland

HEIGHT 70–75 cm (28–30 in)

COLOUR Orange and white; brindle

Swedish Vallhund

Historically, the Vikings used forerunners of this breed as cattle-herders over 1,000 years ago. Today, Swedish farmers continue to use the hardy dog for farm work. Best suited to an outdoor life, the Vallhund needs a lot of physical exercise.

ORIGIN Sweden

HEIGHT 31–35 cm (12–14 in)

COLOUR Grey; red

Sarplaninac

Previously known as the Illyrian Shepherd Dog, this protective herding breed takes its current name from its native land, the Sarplanina Mountains in Macedonia. With a massive build and high energy levels, this breed is happiest when living and working outdoors.

Light-coloured hairs with dark tips

ORIGIN Macedonia
HEIGHT Over 58 cm (over 23 in)
COLOUR Any solid colour

Tatra Shepherd Dog

Bred to work in the high Tatra Mountains of Poland, this huge herder-protector is territorial, defensive, and fearsome when it senses danger. In contrast, it is gentle and mild-mannered among family members.

ORIGIN Poland
HEIGHT 60–70 cm (24–28 in)
COLOUR White

PLAYING WOLF
Herding dogs sometimes use the "strong eye" method to drive livestock. By keeping a distance and maintaining constant eye contact with their heads lowered, the dogs appear to be hunting. The flock reacts by moving away from what it thinks is a predator.

Many herding dogs use a
"strong eye"
approach to intimidate the flock
and keep it together

Caucasian Shepherd Dog

Also called the Caucasian Ovcharka, this breed was used to guard flocks in the past. With strong protective instincts, the Caucasian Shepherd Dog still makes a good watchdog.

ORIGIN Russia

HEIGHT 67–75 cm (26–30 in)

COLOUR Variety of colours

Square, well-built body

Tibetan Mastiff

This breed's massive body and strong defensive instincts make it an excellent guard dog. In the past, Tibetans would allow these dogs to run free at night to protect the village.

ORIGIN
Tibet, China

HEIGHT
61–65 cm
(24–26 in)

COLOUR
Grey with tan markings; gold; black with tan markings

Tosa

Japanese breeders crossed native fighting dogs with Western dogs, such as the Great Dane, the Bulldog, and the Mastiff, to create the Tosa. This is the largest of all Japanese dog breeds.

ORIGIN Japan

HEIGHT 55–60 cm (22–24 in)

COLOUR Fawn; red; black; brindle

Shar Pei

This Chinese breed is easily recognized by its "hippo-shaped" head, wrinkled skin, and rough-textured fur. Shar Peis can have three coat types: the horse coat (stiff and prickly), the brush coat (smooth), and the rare bear coat (fluffy and longer than the other coat types).

ORIGIN China
HEIGHT 46–51 cm (18–20 in)
COLOUR Variety of colours

Australian Cattle Dog

This breed, also called the Australian Heeler, is hardy, easily trained, and energetic. It loves the outdoors and can work for many hours without a break.

ORIGIN Australia
HEIGHT 43–51 cm (17–20 in)
COLOUR Blue with tan markings; red speckle

Because the Tosa is such a large dog, weighing up to 90.7 kg (200 lb), it is illegal to import this breed into some countries.

Spitz-type dogs

Many of the modern spitz breeds known today originated in Arctic regions and across parts of East Asia. The larger members of this group are often used to pull sleds or carts for transport in remote areas. They are also used for herding, hunting, and guarding. The smaller breeds, on the other hand, are kept solely as pets.

CALL OF THE WILD
Siberian Huskies tend to "talk" – howl, yelp, or whine loudly – rather than bark. This is a distinctly wolflike quality shared by some spitz-type dogs.

What is a spitz?

The name "spitz" (German for "pointed") is used for several breeds of dog that live in the northern Polar regions. Huskies, commonly seen pulling sleds over snow, are spitz-type dogs. Similar breeds are used for hunting and racing.

Thick double coat with woolly undercoat provides warmth, and long, coarse hairs protect the skin

Working spitz

Spitz dogs look a bit like wolves. They are big and strong and can survive freezing temperatures. Many share key physical features with the Siberian Husky (below).

Small, triangular, **erect ears**

Narrow, **pointed muzzle**

MUSHING

Mushing refers to any method of sport or transport powered by dogs. Sled-pulling, dog-sled racing, and skijoring (racing on skis pulled by a dog) are forms of mushing. Alaskan Malamutes, Siberian Huskies, and Samoyeds are all mushing breeds.

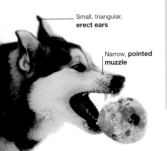

Companion spitz

Smaller than working spitz dogs, pet spitz breeds, such as the Pomeranian, make good watchdogs. However, if bored, they have a tendency to bark.

Pomeranian

FOCUS ON...
FOCUS ON...
FAMOUS DOGS
Some spitz-type dogs have become quite famous.

▶ Hachiko, an Akita in Japan, met his master at the train station every evening. When the owner died, Hachiko continued to visit the station until his death nine years later.

▲ Balto was a Siberian Husky. In 1925, when diphtheria broke out in Alaska, he led the final leg of a 1,084-km (674-mile) run to transport medicine.

Spitz-type dogs

Whether large or small, spitz-type dogs have traits of animals bred for living in cold climates. They have thick double coats, small, pointed ears, and well-furred feet, which all prevent heat loss. These dogs also have tails that curl upwards over their backs

Canadian Eskimo Dog

Also known as the Inuit or Esquimaux Dog, this breed is believed to be one of North America's oldest and rarest breeds. The Canadian Eskimo Dog can tolerate extreme cold.

ORIGIN Canada

HEIGHT 50–70 cm (20–28 in)

COLOUR Any colour

Thick coat with coarse outer hairs

Bushy tail curls over back

Greenland Dog

Arctic people used the Greenland Dog to hunt big animals, such as polar bears and seals. Also used as a sled dog, this breed is often chosen for polar expeditions.

ORIGIN Greenland

HEIGHT 51–68 cm (20–27 in)

COLOUR Any colour

Alaskan Malamute

The Native American Mahlemut people bred this dog to pull heavy loads and travel great distances. Its physical strength and fine sense of direction make it a popular sled dog even today.

ORIGIN USA

HEIGHT 58–71 cm (23–28 in)

COLOUR Variety of colours

American Eskimo Dog

The ancestors of this breed were brought to the USA by Germans who did not want to be parted from their white spitz dogs. This dog comes in three sizes: toy, miniature, and standard.

ORIGIN USA

HEIGHT 23–48 cm (9–19 in)

COLOUR White

Icelandic Sheepdog

A herding dog, the Icelandic Sheepdog is a hardy, muscular breed, useful for rounding up livestock. Long-haired and short-haired varieties exist.

Small, powerful body

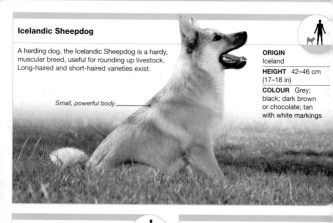

ORIGIN
Iceland

HEIGHT 42–46 cm (17–18 in)

COLOUR Grey; black; dark brown or chocolate; tan with white markings

Papillon

This dainty dog is nicknamed the "butterfly dog" because its ears are said to look like butterfly wings. A favourite among royalty, Papillon-like dogs were often portrayed in 16th-century European court paintings.

ORIGIN
France/Belgium

HEIGHT 20–28 cm (8–11 in)

COLOUR White; black and white; black, tan, and white

German Spitz

There are three sizes of German Spitz: Klein (small), Mittel (standard), and Gross (giant). This breed was popular in Europe in Victorian times.

ORIGIN Germany

HEIGHT 23–50 cm (9–20 in)

COLOUR Variety of colours

Compact body with thick double coat

Schipperke

Flemish river-boatmen used the Schipperke, also known as the Belgian Barge Dog, to guard their boats and hunt rats. This breed barks a lot, but is also fun-loving and energetic.

Wedge-shaped, foxlike head

Tail naturally very short

The Schipperke got its name from the Flemish word "schip", meaning "boat".

Thickset body

ORIGIN Belgium

HEIGHT 25–33 cm (10–13 in)

COLOUR Variety of colours

Pomeranian

Smallest of the spitz-type dogs, the Pomeranian was selectively bred down to "toy" size. It has a soft, fluffy coat with frills around the neck, shoulders, and chest.

ORIGIN Germany

HEIGHT 22–28 cm (9–11 in)

COLOUR Any solid colour (no black or white shading)

Italian Volpino

Italian kings once kept this dog as a pampered pet, while farmers used it as a watchdog. Still serving as a guard dog today, the Italian Volpino alerts bigger dogs to potential trouble with its keen barking.

ORIGIN	Italy
HEIGHT	25–30 cm (10–12 in)
COLOUR	White

Small, round, catlike feet

Finnish Lapphund

The Sami people of Lapland bred the Finnish Lapphund as a reindeer-herder. With the arrival of the snowmobile in the 20th century, it became more popular as a family pet.

ORIGIN	Finland
HEIGHT	44–49 cm (17–19 in)
COLOUR	Any colour

Finnish Spitz

The national dog of Finland, the Finnish Spitz was bred to guide hunters in the direction of small game birds. It is still used in Scandinavia for this purpose today.

ORIGIN	Finland
HEIGHT	39–50 cm (15–20 in)
COLOUR	Red

Swedish Elkhound

Sweden's national dog, the Swedish Elkhound is popular with its country's military forces. It was originally kept for hunting elk, from which it got its name.

ORIGIN Sweden
HEIGHT 52–65 cm (20–26 in)
COLOUR Grey

Strong neck

Narrow muzzle

Norwegian Lundehund

Erect, triangular ears

White markings on neck, chest, and legs

Also called the Norwegian Puffin Dog, the Lundehund was once used as a puffin-hunter. This dog can open its forelegs wider than other dogs, making it particularly agile.

ORIGIN Norway
HEIGHT 32–38 cm (13–15 in)
COLOUR White; grey; black; red

Black Norwegian Elkhound

Originally bred for tracking game, this versatile breed is now used as a sled dog, herder, watchdog, and a family pet.

Pointed ears

ORIGIN Norway
HEIGHT 43–49 cm (17–19 in)
COLOUR Black

Siberian Husky

The peoples of northeastern Siberia used the Siberian Husky as a sled dog. It has great endurance and can tolerate extreme cold. Still popular in the Arctic, this breed is an ideal choice for dogsled-racing.

ORIGIN Siberia
HEIGHT 51–60 cm (20–24 in)
COLOUR Any colour

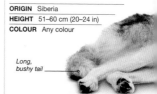

Long, bushy tail

Keeshond

Popular in the Netherlands in the late 18th century, the Keeshond was used as a watchdog and vermin-hunter on riverboats, farms, and barges. It makes a much-loved house dog today.

ORIGIN The Netherlands
HEIGHT 43–46 cm (17–18 in)
COLOUR Black with cream markings

Thick, cream ruff on neck

Well-defined markings

Foxlike head

Thick coat

Samoyed

The Samoyede people of Siberia bred this dog for herding and guarding reindeer. Its easy-going nature made it a popular family pet as well – a position it still enjoys today.

ORIGIN Russia
HEIGHT 46–56 cm (18–22 in)
COLOUR White

Russian-European Laika

Officially recognized as a breed only in the 1940s, this well-built dog has largely been used for hunting bears, wolves, and deer in Russia's northern forests.

Narrow, triangular head

ORIGIN Russia
HEIGHT 48–58 cm (19–23 in)
COLOUR White, cream, or grey; black

Chow Chow

This dog's stocky build, smiling face, and blue-black tongue give it a unique appearance. Two varieties of the Chow Chow exist: rough-coated and smooth-coated.

ORIGIN	China
HEIGHT	46–56 cm (18–22 in)
COLOUR	Cream; gold; red; blue; black

Korean Jindo

Named after the Korean Island of Jindo where it originated, this dog is rarely found outside Korea. It was bred to hunt deer and wild boar, as well as small game, such as rabbits.

ORIGIN	Korea
HEIGHT	46–53 cm (18–21 in)
COLOUR	White; fawn; red; black and tan

Akita

First developed in Japan as a fighting dog, the Akita was later taken to the USA – where larger dogs were preferred – and came to be known as the American Akita. The original smaller dogs, called Akita Inu, are still found in Japan.

ORIGIN	Japan
HEIGHT	61–71 cm (24–28 in)
COLOUR	Any colour

Chow Chow puppies are born with a pink tongue, which darkens to blue-black as they grow up.

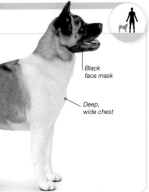

Black face mask

Deep, wide chest

Japanese Shiba Inu

Japan's smallest hunting dog, this breed is considered a "national treasure". The Japanese Shiba Inu makes a lively pet, although it has retained a strong hunting instinct.

ORIGIN Japan

HEIGHT 37–40 cm (15–16 in)

COLOUR White; red; black and tan

"THE LAST GREAT RACE ON EARTH"
Sled dogs need great strength and stamina. In the annual Iditarod Trail Sled Dog Race, teams averaging 16 dogs run for up to six hours at a time without rest, completing 12 hours a day for 10 to 14 days, to cover a total race distance of about 1,770 km (1,100 miles).

Sled dogs can consume up to

10,000 calories

a day, five times the amount
needed by an average human

Hounds

There are two types of dogs in this group: sight hounds and scent hounds. Sight hounds have keen vision and are fast runners. These qualities help them find prey and catch it easily. Scent hounds, on the other hand, have great physical stamina as well as a powerful sense of smell, which they use to find and follow prey.

NOBLE FAVOURITE
The Greyhound is a pack hunter. In the 18th century, the nobility used large, athletic dogs, similar to greyhounds, in sports such as deer and hare coursing.

What is a hound?

Hounds are hunting dogs. They are fast, slim, and strong. There are two main types of hound – scent hounds, who find prey using their keen sense of smell, and sight hounds, who use their sharp vision to hunt.

IN ROYAL COMPANY

Throughout history, hunting has been a regal sport, and hounds appear in many royal paintings and photographs. This picture shows Queen Alexandra, wife of the British King Edward VII, with her pet Borzoi, a sight hound.

Sight hounds

Sometimes called gazehounds, these dogs have excellent eyesight. They hunt by detecting the slightest movement of the quarry. Some catch the prey and kill it themselves, while some only find and hold it until a hunter arrives.

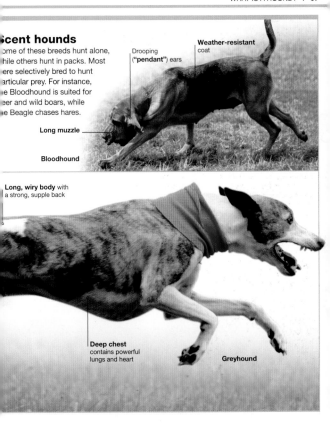

Scent hounds

Some of these breeds hunt alone, while others hunt in packs. Most were selectively bred to hunt a particular prey. For instance, the Bloodhound is suited for deer and wild boars, while the Beagle chases hares.

Drooping (**"pendant"**) ears

Weather-resistant coat

Long muzzle

Bloodhound

Long, wiry body with a strong, supple back

Deep chest contains powerful lungs and heart

Greyhound

Sight hounds

With lightly built but powerful bodies, most sight hounds are easy to recognize. In the past, dogs like these hunted alongside kings and noblemen, as they had the speed to keep up with their horses. Today, sight hounds are used for sports, such as greyhound racing, but most are kept as family pets.

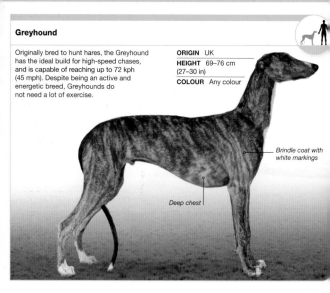

Greyhound

Originally bred to hunt hares, the Greyhound has the ideal build for high-speed chases, and is capable of reaching up to 72 kph (45 mph). Despite being an active and energetic breed, Greyhounds do not need a lot of exercise.

ORIGIN UK

HEIGHT 69–76 cm (27–30 in)

COLOUR Any colour

Brindle coat with white markings

Deep chest

Whippet

The fastest domestic animal for its weight, the Whippet is an energetic dog, capable of speeds up to 56 kph (35 mph). This dog can twist and turn quickly at high speed, which make it perfect for hunting rabbits and hares.

ORIGIN UK

HEIGHT 44–51 cm (17–20 in)

COLOUR Any colour

Rose ears

Irish Wolfhound

The Irish Wolfhound can reach up to 1.8 m (6 ft) when standing on its hind legs. Irish chieftains and kings once used this breed to hunt wolves.

ORIGIN Ireland

HEIGHT 71–86 cm (28–34 in)

COLOUR Variety of colours

Long head with narrow muzzle

Very strong, curved nails

Portuguese Podengo

Three sizes of the Portuguese Podengo exist: Pequeno (small), Medio (medium), and Grande (large). Skilled at hunting rabbits, it is also known as the Portuguese Rabbit Dog.

ORIGIN Portugal

HEIGHT 20–70 cm (8–28 in)

COLOUR White; fawn; black

Italian Greyhound

One of the smallest sight hounds, the Italian Greyhound can reach speeds of 60 kph (40 mph) over short distances. Small greyhound-like dogs were popular among the nobility in the 14th–17th centuries.

ORIGIN Italy

HEIGHT 32–38 cm (13–15 in)

COLOUR Variety of colours

Ibizan Hound

Originally used as a pack dog for hunting rabbits, the Ibizan Hound is unusually quiet when following a scent, which made it especially popular with poachers. Its use in this illegal activity became so common that the breed was banned in some areas.

ORIGIN Spain

HEIGHT 56–74 cm (22–29 in)

COLOUR White; fawn; red

Short, fawn coat

Sloughi

This athletic African dog became known in Europe and the USA only relatively recently. A rare breed, the Sloughi makes a pleasant and loyal companion.

ORIGIN	North Africa
HEIGHT	61–72 cm (24–28 in)
COLOUR	Fawn

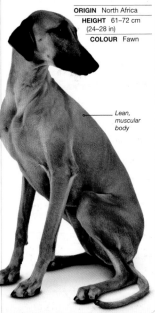

Lean, muscular body

Pharaoh Hound

This hound resembles hunting dogs illustrated in the art of ancient Egypt. Because of this and its slim and graceful appearance, its name was changed from Maltese Rabbit Dog to Pharaoh Hound.

ORIGIN	Malta
HEIGHT	53–63 cm (21–25 in)
COLOUR	Dark tan

Greyhounds are the

fastest dogs

on Earth. They can run at speeds
of up to 72 kph (45 mph)

DOG RACING
Greyhounds are popularly used in dog racing, a common dog sporting event. These dogs chase a mechanical a "lure", until they cross the finishing line. This sport developed from coursing, a hunting technique in which greyhounds would chase down and capture prey.

Basenji

Primarily a hunting dog, the Basenji locates its prey using both sight and scent. These dogs were made to wear bells on their collars to scare the animals they were tracking into a hunter's net.

ORIGIN	Central Africa
HEIGHT	40–43 cm (16–17 in)
COLOUR	Variety of colours

Also known as the "barkless dog", the Basenji, when excited, makes a noise that sounds like a yodel.

Saluki

The Saluki is an athletic dog that was used to hunt gazelle, often with a falcon as a partner. It can run at speeds of 55 kph (40 mph). There are two coat types – smooth and feathered.

ORIGIN	Persia
HEIGHT	58–71 cm (23–28 in)
COLOUR	Variety of colours

Borzoi

The Russian nobility used this large, silky-haired dog to hunt wolves. Outside Russia, it has been bred as a companion for many years. However, it needs plenty of space and exercise as well as regular grooming.

ORIGIN	Russia
HEIGHT	68–74 cm (27–29 in)
COLOUR	Variety of colours

Afghan Hound

Once used to hunt hares and wolves, the Afghan Hound is now better known for its luxurious coat, and is a favourite at dog shows.

ORIGIN	Afghanistan
HEIGHT	63–74 cm (25–29 in)
COLOUR	Any colour

Long, gold coat shorter over the back

Strong feet, covered with thick, long hair

Scent hounds

As their name suggests, scent hounds are known for their ability to hunt by smelling out their quarry. Their noses are packed with sensors that allow them to follow a scent trail, even if it is days old. Most dogs in this group are characterized by loose, moist lips and long, pendant ears.

Bluetick Coonhound

This athletic breed gets its name from the spots (known as ticking) on its dark blue coat and the fact that it is mainly used to track raccoons and opossums.

Ticking on coat gives distinctive colour

ORIGIN	USA
HEIGHT	53–69 cm (21–27 in)
COLOUR	Blue

Plott Hound

Well-built body

The Plott family, who came to the USA from Germany, bred the first Plott Hound in the 1750s. This powerful dog is used for hunting raccoons, although it also hunts big cats, bears, coyotes, and wild boars.

ORIGIN	USA
HEIGHT	51–64 cm (20–25 in)
COLOUR	Brindle

Otterhound

This strong, energetic, and shaggy-coated dog
is built for running. Once used to hunt otters,
the Otterhound population declined sharply
when its quarry became a protected species.

ORIGIN	UK
HEIGHT	61–69 cm (24–27 in)
COLOUR	Any colour

The Otterhound
is rare: fewer than
60 puppies are
registered by the
UK Kennel Club
each year.

Beagle

Tan markings on face

Once used for hunting, the Beagle is a sturdy and lively breed. As a police and security dog, it is nowadays used to sniff out illegal items, such as drugs and explosives.

ORIGIN UK
HEIGHT 33–40 cm (13–16 in)
COLOUR Variety of colours

Ariégeois

This dog is named after the dry, rocky French region from which it comes. Unusually for a pack hound, it is also content to be a family pet.

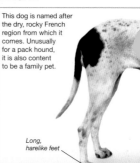

Long, harelike feet

English Foxhound

Originally an athletic and powerful hound that hunted foxes for hours at a time, the English Foxhound needs plenty of exercise if kept as a household pet. It remains playful and energetic even into old age.

ORIGIN UK
HEIGHT 58–64 cm (23–25 in)
COLOUR Variety of colours

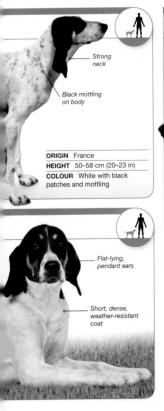

Strong
neck

Black mottling
on body

ORIGIN France

HEIGHT 50–58 cm (20–23 in)

COLOUR White with black
patches and mottling

Flat-lying,
pendant ears

Short, dense,
weather-resistant
coat

Poitevin

This hound was once used to hunt
wolves in packs, but today tracks deer
and wild boars. The Poitevin has great stamina
and is even able to trail its quarry through water.

Well-muscled
body

ORIGIN France

HEIGHT 62–72 cm (24–28 in)

COLOUR Tan and white; black, tan, and white

Basset Bleu de Gascogne

Slow, but very determined, this short-legged hound was once used to track wolves, deer, and wild boars. Today it is more often seen as a household pet.

ORIGIN France

HEIGHT 30–38 cm (12–15 in)

COLOUR Black, tan, and white

Long, pendant ears

Black-and-white, mottled coat with dark patches

Basset Fauve de Bretagne

With a strong sense of smell, this breed is excellent at tracking hares, rabbits, and foxes. Today it is also used for search-and-rescue work.

ORIGIN France

HEIGHT 32–38 cm (13–15 in)

COLOUR Gold

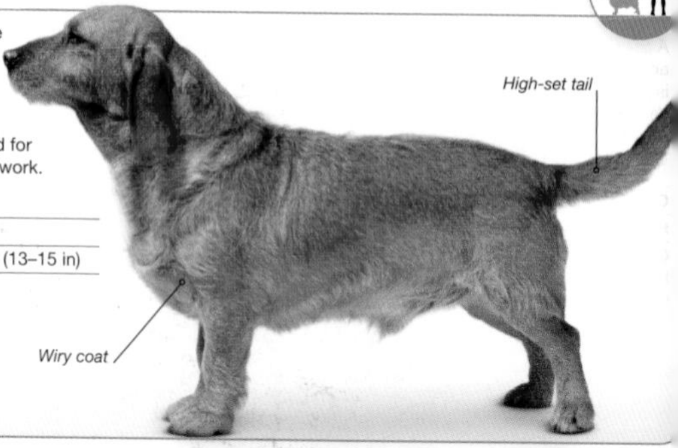

High-set tail

Wiry coat

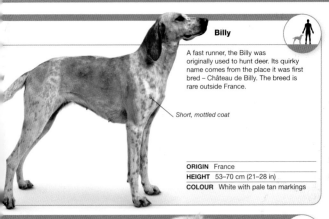

Billy

A fast runner, the Billy was originally used to hunt deer. Its quirky name comes from the place it was first bred – Château de Billy. The breed is rare outside France.

Short, mottled coat

ORIGIN	France
HEIGHT	53–70 cm (21–28 in)
COLOUR	White with pale tan markings

Briquet Griffon Vendéen

A pack hound used for hunting wild boars and roe deer, the Briquet Griffon Vendéen is a tough breed. It got its name from the Vendée area of Western France, where it originated.

ORIGIN	France
HEIGHT	48–55 cm (19–22 in)
COLOUR	Fawn; black and tan; black and white; black, tan, and white; gold and white

Long, shaggy coat

French White and Black Hound

Strong and powerful, the French White and Black Hound is used to hunt roe deer. Though friendly in nature, it is best suited to life among members of its pack.

ORIGIN France

HEIGHT 62–72 cm (24–28 in)

COLOUR Black and white

Petit Basset Griffon Vendéen

With lots of energy and excellent stamina, the Petit Basset Griffon Vendéen can hunt all day long. Its thick, rough coat makes this breed ideal for hunting in dense scrub.

Deep chest

Basset Hound

This breed can search, track, flush out, and pursue hares, foxes, and pheasants on its own or in small packs. Its name comes from the French word "bas" (meaning "low"), which refers to the Basset Hound's low-slung body and short legs.

ORIGIN France

HEIGHT 33–38 cm (13–15 in)

COLOUR Variety of colours

Of all dogs, Basset Hounds have the longest ears relative to their overall body size.

ORIGIN
France

HEIGHT 33–38 cm
(13–15 in)

COLOUR White with
dark markings

*Pendant ears
turned inwards*

Short legs

Great Anglo-French
Tricolour Hound

The word "Great" in this breed's name
is not a reference to the dog's size, but to the
size of its quarry. With strong muscles and good
stamina, this tricoloured hound is used to hunt
large game, such as red deer.

ORIGIN France

HEIGHT 62–72 cm
(24–28 in)

COLOUR Black,
tan, and white

*Short, coarse,
tricoloured coat*

Bloodhound

Known for its excellent tracking skills,
the Bloodhound is capable of picking up
a scent that is as much as several days old.
Its keen sense of smell makes it suitable for
hunting, police work, and rescue missions.

William the
Conqueror brought
dogs similar to the
Bloodhound to
England in 1066.

ORIGIN Belgium

HEIGHT 58–69 cm (23–27 in)

COLOUR Liver and tan; black and tan

Segugio Italiano

Usually a calm and quiet dog, the Segugio Italiano is known for its typically high-pitched bark when it is hunting. This breed can run long distances at great speed.

Smooth, red coat

Low-set, pendant ears

Oval feet

ORIGIN Italy
HEIGHT 48–59 cm (19–23 in)
COLOUR Gold; red; black and tan

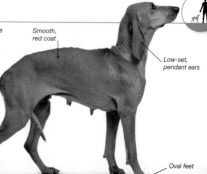

Laufhund

This dog, also known as the Swiss Hound, has a long muzzle, which it uses to track hares, foxes, and roe deer. There are four types of Laufhund, each having a different coat colour – Jura, Schwyz, Bernese, and Lucerne.

ORIGIN Switzerland
HEIGHT 47–59 cm (19–23 in)
COLOUR Black and tan; orange and white; blue; black and white

Hanoverian Scent Hound

Bred and still used to track wounded game, such as deer and wild boars, the Hanoverian Scent Hound works alone or in pairs.

Dachshund

Most countries recognize two sizes of the Dachshund: the miniature and the standard. Because of its long body and short legs, it has earned the nicknames "sausage dog" and "weiner".

ORIGIN Germany

HEIGHT 13–23 cm (5–9 in)

COLOUR Variety of colours

Long-haired coat

ORIGIN Germany

HEIGHT 48–55 cm (19–22 in)

COLOUR Brindle

Dobermann

Reportedly named after the German tax official who first bred it, the Dobermann is thought to include German Shepherd, Greyhound, Rottweiler, and Weimaraner in its ancestry. It is a good watchdog.

ORIGIN Germany

HEIGHT 65–69 cm (26–27 in)

COLOUR Fawn; blue; brown; black and tan

Schillerstovare

Named after its breeder, farmer Per Schiller, the Schillerstovare has great hunting stamina and speed, especially over snow. It tracks alone, using its deep-sounding bark to guide hunters to the quarry.

Thick, black saddle

Strong, long neck

Short, glossy, tan coat with thick undercoat

ORIGIN Sweden
HEIGHT 49–61 cm (19–24 in)
COLOUR Black and tan

Norwegian Hound

Also known as the Dunker, the Norwegian Hound is a hardy breed. It can track hares through snow in temperatures as low as −15°C (−59°F).

Blue, marbled back

ORIGIN Norway
HEIGHT 47–55 cm (19–22 in)
COLOUR Black, tan, and white; blue marbled; tan and white

Hygen Hound

Bred to hunt for long periods in the snowy Arctic, the Hygen Hound has boundless energy. This means it needs a lot of exercise.

White tip on tail

ORIGIN Norway

HEIGHT 47–58 cm (19–23 in)

COLOUR Black and tan; red and white; tan and white

Polish Hound

Used for hunting a wide variety of game in the thick forests of Poland, this rare breed is renowned for its tracking abilities, even when running at high speed.

ORIGIN Poland

HEIGHT 55–65 cm (22–26 in)

COLOUR Black and tan

Spanish Hound

Also known as the Sabueso Español, the Spanish Hound is used mainly to hunt for hares in mountainous regions. It hunts alone, rather than in a pack, and can work all day and in a wide range of temperatures.

ORIGIN Spain

HEIGHT 48–57 cm (19–22 in)

COLOUR Gold and white

Long, straight muzzle

Male Spanish Hounds are taller than females by at least 5 cm (2 in).

Dogs have more than

300 million

smell-detecting cells, while
humans have only 6 million

NOSE POWER
The part of a dog's brain that identifies scent is 40 times larger than that of a human's. Some of the more unusual things dogs can be trained to sniff out include certain minerals and metals, bed bug infestations, bacteria, and even the presence of some illnesses.

Hellenic Hound

Once used for hunting boars and hares, the Hellenic Hound has an athletic build and needs plenty of space to run around. This dog is known for its musical voice that can be heard over long distances.

ORIGIN Greece

HEIGHT 45–55 cm (18–22 in)

COLOUR Black and tan

Drop ears with rounded tips

Short, smooth coat

Transylvanian Hound

This hardy breed's ability to tolerate extreme climates made it a popular game-hunter among the kings and princes of Hungary. It is known for its good sense of direction.

ORIGIN Hungary

HEIGHT 55–65 cm (22–26 in)

COLOUR Black and tan

Bosnian Rough-coated Hound

This dog used to be known as the Illyrian Hound. Its most striking feature is its coat. The thick, coarse hair helps it to work in dense undergrowth during cold winters.

Dark red, drop ears

ORIGIN Bosnia and Herzegovina

HEIGHT 45–56 cm (18–22 in)

COLOUR Black and tan; black, tan, and white

Coarse, short coat

Clearly defined tan markings

Serbian Hound

It is believed that Serbian Hounds were once used to set off buried land mines to save the lives of children.

Black mantle

Rhodesian Ridgeback

Also called the African Lion Hound, this breed was once used in packs to hunt lions. The name "Ridgeback" refers to a distinctive ridge of hair along its back that grows in the opposite direction to the rest of its coat.

ORIGIN	Zimbabwe
HEIGHT	61–69 cm (24–27 in)
COLOUR	Red

A pack hunter, the Serbian Hound can track game of all sizes, from rabbits to elks and boars. Its gentle nature makes it a good companion dog.

ORIGIN	Serbia
HEIGHT	44–56 cm (17–22 in)
COLOUR	Black and tan

Terriers

Traditionally used as hunting dogs for working men, terriers are well known for being tough and fearless. The smaller dogs in the group were originally used as vermin-hunters, while their larger cousins were used to hunt badgers and otters. Nowadays, the majority of terriers are kept as pets and watchdogs.

WHAT'S IN A NAME?
Some small terriers are known by the types of animals they originally hunted: for example, the Rat Terrier.

What is a terrier?

The name "terrier" comes from the Latin word "terra", which means earth. The dogs in this group like to dig, and so they are well suited for hunting animals such as rats, mice, and rabbits, which live or hide underground.

Digging holes

Terriers have a natural instinct for digging holes. This means that, if you don't watch them, pet terriers can make a big mess in the garden!

A Jack Russell Terrier, known to be a keen digger

SIZE DIFFERENCES

Terriers – such as the Airedale (above) – that were bred to hunt large game, or to be used as security dogs, are big and powerful.

In the past, terriers were crossed with bulldogs to create muscular breeds for dog fighting. The Staffordshire Bull Terrier (above) is one such example.

Many small terriers, such as the Yorkshire (above), Scottish, Norfolk, and West Highland, were first bred to hunt rats and mice.

Independent streak

Most terriers are intelligent and friendly, but they can also be stubborn, with minds of their own. They will keep chasing prey until they catch it, and they are not afraid to stand up to bigger dogs.

A Fox Terrier (right) playing with a Boxer (left)

Full of life

Terriers make perfect pets because they are affectionate and quick to react to what's going on around them. They also have lots of energy for running, playing, chasing, and, of course, digging holes.

A playful West Highland White Terrier

Terriers

Originally, terriers were bred to hunt animals that live underground. These dogs are, therefore, small in size, but tough, confident, and full of energy. Later, breeders also created terriers with large, powerful bodies, to be suitable for more than just hunting.

Boston Terrier

Native to the USA, the Boston Terrier is a mix of Bulldog and several terrier breeds, including the white English Terrier (now extinct). Intelligent and alert, this terrier makes an ideal pet.

ORIGIN USA
HEIGHT 38–43 cm (15–17 in)
COLOUR Black; brindle

Erect, pointed ears

Short muzzle

White markings on black coat

A distinctive black-and-white "tuxedo" look has led to the Boston Terrier's nickname, "American Gentleman".

Parson Russell Terrier

This breed is one of two similar types of terrier originally grouped under the name Jack Russell Terrier. The longer-legged type is today known as the Parson Russell Terrier.

ORIGIN UK

HEIGHT 33–36 cm (13–14 in)

COLOUR White with black and/or tan markings

West Highland White Terrier

The Scots originally bred this dog to hunt foxes, badgers, and vermin. Its thick, white coat allows it to be easily seen as it chases its quarry through the undergrowth.

ORIGIN UK

HEIGHT 25–28 cm (10–11 in)

COLOUR White

Yorkshire Terrier

People often describe this popular breed as big dogs in small bodies. This is because, despite its miniature size, a Yorkshire Terrier is not intimidated by larger dogs.

ORIGIN UK

HEIGHT 20–23 cm (8–9 in)

COLOUR Blue with tan markings

Airedale Terrier

The largest member of its group, the Airedale is known as the "king of terriers". Originally used to hunt otters, this powerful breed is nowadays commonly used for police and military work.

Tail held high when alert

Hard, dense, and wiry coat

ORIGIN UK

HEIGHT 56–61 cm (22–24 in)

COLOUR Black and tan

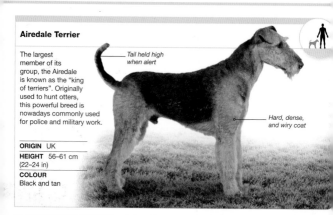

Scottish Terrier

Also known as Scotties, these terriers were bred to hunt vermin. One dog, called Billy, is said to have killed 100 rats in seven minutes. Loving and alert, Scottish Terriers also make excellent family pets.

ORIGIN UK

HEIGHT 25–28 cm (10–11 in)

COLOUR Gold; black

Body thickset, but not heavy

Skye Terrier

The Skye Terrier's long-haired coat takes several years to grow to full adult length and it requires a lot of grooming. Once a skilled vermin-hunter, this breed makes a devoted pet.

ORIGIN UK

HEIGHT Up to 26 cm (10 in)

COLOUR Cream; grey; fawn; black

English Toy Terrier

Valued for their rat-hunting abilities, English Toy Terriers once competed in "rat-pits". These events involved timing how long it took them to kill a given number of rats.

ORIGIN UK

HEIGHT 25–30 cm (10–12 in)

COLOUR Black and tan

Candle-flame ears

Dark, almond-shaped eyes

The English Toy Terrier is now rare and in danger of becoming extinct.

Border Terrier

Bred in the 18th century, this terrier was large enough to hunt with hounds, but small enough to flush prey from its den if necessary. It is known for its friendly character.

ORIGIN UK

HEIGHT 25–28 cm (10–11 in)

COLOUR Gold; red; blue and tan; black and tan

Welsh Terrier

This hardy and agile terrier was once used in packs for hunting foxes, badgers, and otters. Courageous and intelligent, the Welsh Terrier is always eager to please, making it an easy-to-train dog.

ORIGIN UK

HEIGHT Up to 39 cm (15 in)

COLOUR Black and tan

Bull Terrier

A mix of the Bulldog and various terrier breeds, the Bull Terrier was originally created to be a fighting dog. Despite having the ideal strength and build for this, it lacked the necessary aggression.

ORIGIN UK

HEIGHT 53–56 cm (21–22 in)

COLOUR Variety of colours

Staffordshire Bull Terrier

Bred for dog-fighting in the 19th century, the Staffordshire Bull Terrier is known for its courage. Today, it has become one of the UK's most popular pet breeds.

Powerful, muscular body

ORIGIN UK

HEIGHT 36–41 cm (14–16 in)

COLOUR Variety of colours

Bedlington Terrier

One of the more unusual-looking terriers, the Bedlington has a soft, woolly coat that gives it a unique, lamblike appearance. Its ancestry, which includes the Whippet, has given it speed for hunting and a gentle nature.

Thin, velvety, drop ears

ORIGIN UK

HEIGHT 40–43 cm (16–17 in)

COLOUR Gold; liver; blue

The Bedlington has "filbert-shaped ears", so named because they resemble the leaves of the filbert (hazelnut) tree.

Kerry Blue Terrier

The Kerry Blue Terrier is Ireland's national dog. It has a distinctive soft, dense, wavy coat. It is born black, but due to a gene that causes colour fading, its coat changes to blue by the time it is two years old.

ORIGIN Ireland

HEIGHT 46–48 cm (18–19 in)

COLOUR Blue

Soft, wavy coat sheds very little

Beard covers strong jaw and black nose

Affenpinscher

This dog is loved for its mischievous nature. The Affenpinscher's name (meaning "monkey–terrier" in German) comes from its flattened face with a short muzzle, which gives it an apelike appearance.

ORIGIN Germany

HEIGHT 24–28 cm (9–11 in)

COLOUR Black

Blunt muzzle

Kromfohrländer

A modern breed, the Kromfohrländer gets its name from the Krom Fohr area in western Germany where it first appeared. Though rare around the world, the breed makes a good watchdog, rat-catcher, and companion.

ORIGIN Germany

HEIGHT 38–46 cm (15–18 in)

COLOUR White with tan markings

Cesky Terrier

Also known as the Bohemian Terrier, this dog is considered a national breed in the Czech Republic. Bred in the 1940s, the Cesky Terrier is highly skilled at hunting in packs or on its own. It also makes a good watchdog and pet.

Slightly wavy, silky coat

ORIGIN	Czech Republic
HEIGHT	25–32 cm (10–13 in)
COLOUR	Grey; blue; liver

Russian Black Terrier

The Soviet army developed this breed in the 1940s as a strong and hardy dog suitable for use in the armed forces. The Russian Black Terrier's large and robust body comes from its parent breeds, which include Rottweilers, Giant Schnauzers, and Airedale Terriers.

Strong, muscular body

Thick coat

ORIGIN	Russia
HEIGHT	66–77 cm (26–30 in)
COLOUR	Black

Long hair on face forms beard

A much-loved, breed, the Cesky Terrier has featured on postage stamps of its native land, the Czech Republic.

Japanese Terrier

Also called Nippon Terriers, these friendly dogs make excellent companions. However, they are quite rare, both in their native land and around the world.

High-set ears

ORIGIN	Japan
HEIGHT	30–33 cm (12–13 in)
COLOUR	White with black markings; black, tan, and white

Australian Terrier

This dog was bred from various terrier dogs, including Skye, Yorkshire, and Scottish Terriers. An energetic dog, it was originally developed to hunt rabbits and rats.

ORIGIN	Australia
HEIGHT	Up to 26 cm (10 in)
COLOUR	Red; blue with tan

Erect ears

Harsh, straight, dense coat

Small, compact feet with black nails

Franklin D Roosevelt's Scottish Terrier, Fala, is the only presidential pet honoured with a statue beside that of his master

CONSTANT COMPANION
Accompanying his master almost everywhere, Fala became a celebrity himself. Some even called him the "most photographed dog in the world". Always at the President's side, Fala was an important part of Roosevelt's public image.

Gundogs

Dogs in this group were developed to accompany and assist hunters with guns, rather than chase and capture prey as hounds do. Gundogs are broadly divided into three groups based on the tasks they perform. Pointers and setters find prey; spaniels drive out game from hiding; and retrievers fetch fallen prey and bring it back to the hunter.

"SOFT-MOUTHED"
The retrievers, good at collecting fallen prey, are known to have "soft" mouths, which means they are able to carry an object without damaging it.

What is a gundog?

Gundogs were first used when people began to hunt game (usually birds) using firearms. These breeds are also called "sporting" dogs. They all hunt by scent, and they can help a hunter in three ways – by pointing, flushing, and retrieving prey.

Pointing

When gundogs find game they show the hunter where it is. Pointers, such as the English Pointer (left), stay very still with their nose, body, and tail in a line, "pointing" to the prey. Setters crouch, or "set", in the direction of the creature's scent.

An English Pointer in a distinct pointing pose

Flushing

Flushing is a process by which gundogs drive out prey, especially birds, from their hiding places and force them to fly up so they can be shot. Spaniels are bred and trained to flush game birds on land, and also in shallow water.

A Brittany Spaniel flushing

MULTITASKING

Some breeds, such as the Hungarian Vizsla (left), German Pointer, and Weimaraner, are trained to do all three jobs of pointing, flushing, and retrieving prey. These are called HPR (hunt, point, and retrieve) dogs.

Retrieving

Once a bird has been shot, retrievers pick it up and take to the hunter. They have keen eyesight, which enables them to follow the prey to wherever it falls. They then collect it without causing damage.

A Golden Retriever fetching a shot bird

Gundogs

Traditionally, dogs helped to spot and chase game during a hunt. When the use of guns became popular, a different type of dog was needed for specific tasks and to work more closely with hunters. Gundogs were bred for such jobs.

Labrador Retriever

Canadian fishermen once used ancestors of this water-loving breed to pull in their nets and retrieve escaping fish. Today, the Labrador Retriever makes an ideal family pet, search-and-rescue dog, and guide dog for the blind.

ORIGIN	Canada
HEIGHT	55–57 cm (22 in)
COLOUR	Black; chocolate; yellow

Short, water-resistant coat

American Cocker Spaniel

This spaniel is smaller than the English Cocker Spaniel from which it originated. Although this dog is today more common as a pet, it is said to be still capable of performing hunting tasks.

ORIGIN USA

HEIGHT 34–39 cm (13–15 in)

COLOUR Any colour

The name "cocker" comes from this breed's skill in hunting woodcock, a popular game bird.

Chesapeake Bay Retriever

The toughest of the retriever breeds, this hardy dog can work for long hours in harsh weather. The Chesapeake Bay Retriever's thick, double-layered coat protects it in rough, icy waters, a useful characteristic given that it is used to hunt waterfowl.

ORIGIN USA
HEIGHT 53–66 cm (21–26 in)
COLOUR
Gold; red; brown

English Setter

The oldest of the setter breeds, the English Setter has a silky, white coat flecked with colour, which is given the name "belton". Its calm, reliable nature makes it a good family pet.

ORIGIN UK
HEIGHT 61–64 cm (24–25 in)
COLOUR Orange and white; liver and white; black and white

Sussex Spaniel

Pendant ears covered with long, silky hair

Round feet with feathering between toes

Bred to hunt in dense undergrowth, the Sussex Spaniel, unlike other spaniel breeds, barks while working so the hunter knows exactly where it is.

ORIGIN UK
HEIGHT 38–41 cm (14–16 in)
COLOUR Liver

Black hairs create blue belton pattern

English Springer Spaniel

This gundog's name comes from its original role – to "spring", or startle, birds into the air. Energetic and tough, the English Springer Spaniel can work outdoors, even in difficult weather or freezing water.

ORIGIN UK

HEIGHT 46–56 cm (18–22 in)

COLOUR Black and white; liver and white

Thick, straight, weather-resistant coat

English Pointer

Hunters have long used this swift and obedient dog for tracking and pointing. Simply known as the Pointer in the UK, the breed still has strong hunting instincts.

ORIGIN UK

HEIGHT 61–69 cm (24–27 in)

COLOUR Variety of colours

Golden Retriever

One of the most popular breeds in the world, the Golden Retriever has a "soft" mouth, which means it can carry fragile items with its teeth without damaging them. Eager to please, this breed is often used to assist people with disabilities.

ORIGIN UK

HEIGHT 51–61 cm (20–24 in)

COLOUR Gold; cream

Drop ears

Long, silky coat

Irish Setter

The Irish call this attractive canine the Modder Rhu ("red dog"). The name refers to the breed's characteristic long, silky, glossy, red coat.

ORIGIN Ireland

HEIGHT 64–69 cm (25–27 in)

COLOUR Red

French Gascony Pointer

One of the oldest pointer breeds, this hunting dog comes from southwest France. People continue to use it as a tracking dog. Affectionate and loyal, the French Gascony Pointer also makes an excellent family pet.

ORIGIN France

HEIGHT 56–69 cm (22–27 in)

COLOUR Brown; brown and white

Blue Picardy Spaniel

This hardy water
dog is used mainly as
a pointer and retriever,
especially in marshlands.
Its easy-going nature makes
it a good companion but
an unsuitable guard dog.

Grey-black speckling

ORIGIN	France
HEIGHT	57–60 cm (23–24 in)
COLOUR	Blue with darker patches

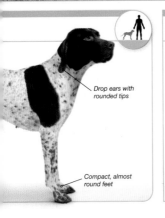

*Drop ears with
rounded tips*

*Compact, almost
round feet*

French Spaniel

In its native France, this intelligent and
handsome dog is considered the original
hunting spaniel. One of the larger spaniel
breeds, the French Spaniel makes
a good flushing, retrieving,
and pointing dog.

Pendant ears

ORIGIN	France
HEIGHT	55–61cm (22–24 in)
COLOUR	White and brown

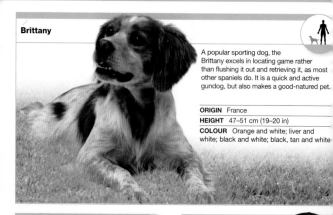

Brittany

A popular sporting dog, the Brittany excels in locating game rather than flushing it out and retrieving it, as most other spaniels do. It is a quick and active gundog, but also makes a good-natured pet.

ORIGIN France

HEIGHT 47–51 cm (19–20 in)

COLOUR Orange and white; liver and white; black and white; black, tan and white

Large Munsterlander

A versatile gundog that is easy to train, the Large Munsterlander also enjoys human company and makes a good family pet.

ORIGIN Germany

HEIGHT 58–65 cm (23–26 in)

COLOUR Black and white

Long, dense coat

German Pointer

An ideal hunting breed, the German Pointer is good at tracking, retrieving, and pointing. There are three types of coat: wire-haired, long-haired, and short-haired.

ORIGIN Germany

HEIGHT 53–64 cm (21–25 in)

COLOUR Liver; liver and white; black; black and white

Spoon-shaped feet

Weimaraner

This 19th-century breed was originally called the Weimer Pointer. The Weimaraner is nicknamed the "grey ghost" because of its unusual silver-grey coat colour and light-coloured eyes. Coats are either long or short.

ORIGIN Germany

HEIGHT 56–69 cm (22–27 in)

COLOUR Grey

Nose matches coat colour

Italian Spinone

Long moustache blends into beard

This northern Italian breed was once the region's most popular hunting dog. Although it is still used to track and retrieve game today, the Italian Spinone is well loved as a companion dog, due to its sweet temper and loyal nature.

ORIGIN Italy

HEIGHT 58–70 cm (23–28 in)

COLOUR White; white and orange; white and brown

Tapering tail with white tip

Lagotto Romagnolo

This northern Italian breed was originally
used as a retrieving dog. It was later trained
to track and find truffles, a type of edible
fungus used in fine cuisine.

*Woolly coat
forms tight curls*

ORIGIN Italy

HEIGHT 41–48 cm (16–19 in)

COLOUR White; gold; brown;
orange and white

Cesky Fousek

An efficient pointing dog, the Cesky
Fousek is a wire-haired breed with strong
hunting instincts. It is popular in its native
land but uncommon elsewhere.

ORIGIN Czech
Republic

HEIGHT 58–66 cm
(23–26 in)

COLOUR Brown;
brown and white

Kooikerhondje

The Kooikerhondje is also called the
Dutch Decoy Spaniel. The name comes
from its unusual hunting method of silently
luring waterfowl into "kooien" (traps) by
running and waving its flaglike tail.

ORIGIN The Netherlands

HEIGHT 35–40 cm
(14–16 in)

COLOUR
Orange and white

Spanish Water Dog

Although mainly used to retrieve water birds, the Spanish Water Dog is also used to herd sheep, moving them between their summer and winter pastures.

ORIGIN Spain

HEIGHT 40–50 cm (16–20 in)

COLOUR White; black; brown; brown and white; black and white

Curly, woolly coat

The Spanish Water Dog is a good swimmer, in spite of its small size and thick, woolly coat.

Portuguese Water Dog

This breed is good at both retrieving and swimming. These skills once helped it pull fishermen's nets from the water. Its coat may be long and wavy or short and curly.

ORIGIN Portugal

HEIGHT 43–57 cm (17–22 in)

COLOUR White; brown; black; black and white; brown and white

Hungarian Vizsla

A versatile hunting dog, the Hungarian Vizsla nearly died out during World War II. However, it has since regained popularity, not only for its use in hunting but also as a family companion.

ORIGIN Hungary

HEIGHT 53–64 cm (21–25 in)

COLOUR Gold

A dog can shake off up to 70 per cent
of water from its fur in roughly

4 seconds

DRYING OFF
Many gundogs are good swimmers and spend a lot of time in the water. Shaking vigorously helps them keep their coats dry in order to stay warm. Although many other mammals also shake off water, dogs are said to be the most efficient at drying themselves in this way.

Companion dogs

Almost all dog breeds, even if bred for specific purposes, make excellent companions. However, there are some dogs that were developed solely as pets. These are known as companion breeds. Chosen mainly for their appearance, these dogs find a place with owners of all ages.

HANDBAG DOGS
A Chihuahua is small enough to fit into a handbag, but it cannot be treated like a toy. It needs just as much exercise as a larger dog.

What is a companion dog?

Companion dogs are pets, although some were once working dogs. This group includes breeds that are meant solely to provide companionship. They look good and are easy to train. People have kept them for years

Best friends

At one time, companion dogs were the spoiled toys of nobility and royalty. Today, they serve as loyal friends, especially to children

A Dalmatian playing with a young boy

Unusual appearance

Over the years, people have bred companion dogs to look a certain way. Some are particularly appealing, such as the Pekingese (right) with its big eyes. Some breeds have curious features. The Peruvian Hairless, for instance, has hardly any hair. It also has fewer teeth than other breeds.

A Pekingese, known for its humanlike face

Toy versions

Many companion dogs are selectively bred to create smaller versions of larger dogs used for herding or hunting. For example, the Standard Poodle is a gundog. However, its scaled-downed versions – the Miniature Poodle and the Toy Poodle – are companion breeds.

Standard Poodle

Miniature Poodle

Toy Poodle

Companion dogs

Chosen for their looks or unusual appearance, companion dogs act as friends that give and demand affection and adapt to family life. These dogs were originally bred to be decorative, friendly, and small enough to be able to sit on their owner's lap

Chihuahua

The smallest dog breed in the world, the Chihuahua is highly intelligent and possessive, which makes it an excellent watchdog. Believed to have Chinese origins, it got its name from the Mexican state of Chihuahua where it became popular in the 1890s.

Batlike ears

Smooth, glossy topcoat

ORIGIN Mexico

HEIGHT 15–23 cm (6–9 in)

COLOUR Any solid colour except white

Mexican Hairless

The Mexican Hairless was once regarded as a sacred dog. It nearly became extinct, but in the mid-20th century efforts were made to revive its declining numbers. It is known for its loyalty.

ORIGIN Mexico

HEIGHT 25–60 cm (10–24 in)

COLOUR Red; liver; fawn; grey; black

Firm, slender neck

Havanese

It is believed that Italian or Spanish traders brought the ancestors of the Havanese with them to Cuba. The dog is named after Havana, the nation's capital. It makes a good family pet.

ORIGIN Cuba

HEIGHT 23–28 cm (9–11 in)

COLOUR Any colour

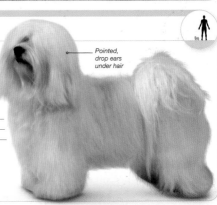

Pointed, drop ears under hair

Peruvian Hairless

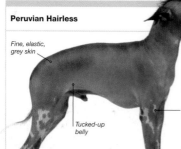

Fine, elastic, grey skin

The Peruvian Hairless breed can be one of three sizes: miniature, medio, and grande. It is characterized by hairlessness, fewer teeth than other breeds, and fine skin that is easily sunburned. This dog is gentle and affectionate towards its owners, but shy with strangers.

Pink patches on legs

Tucked-up belly

ORIGIN	Peru
HEIGHT	25–65 cm (10–26 in)
COLOUR	Cream; grey; dark brown; black

Cavalier King Charles Spaniel

A perfect family pet, the Cavalier King Charles Spaniel is an outgoing dog and loves human company. It has an easy-going nature and is good with children.

ORIGIN	UK
HEIGHT	30–33 cm (12–13 in)
COLOUR	Red; gold and white; black and tan; black, tan, and white

Large, dark eyes

Bichon Frise

It is said that the Bichon Frise was originally exported from Tenerife to France, because of which it is also known as the Tenerife Dog. It is a small, fun-loving dog, with a dense, but non-shedding, coat.

ORIGIN	Mediterranean
HEIGHT	23–28 cm (9–11 in)
COLOUR	White

Poodle

The Poodle has always been a popular companion dog. Its special feature is its non-shedding coat, which makes it an ideal choice for people with allergies. There are three sizes of Poodle: toy, miniature, and medium.

ORIGIN France

HEIGHT 28–45 cm (11–18 in)

COLOUR All solid colours

Pendant ears

Topcoat coarser than soft, dense undercoat

French Bulldog

Always ready for fun, the French Bulldog makes an excellent companion. The sturdy little dog was bred from the British Toy Bulldog in the 19th century.

ORIGIN France

HEIGHT 28–33 cm (11–13 in)

COLOUR Fawn; brindle; black and white

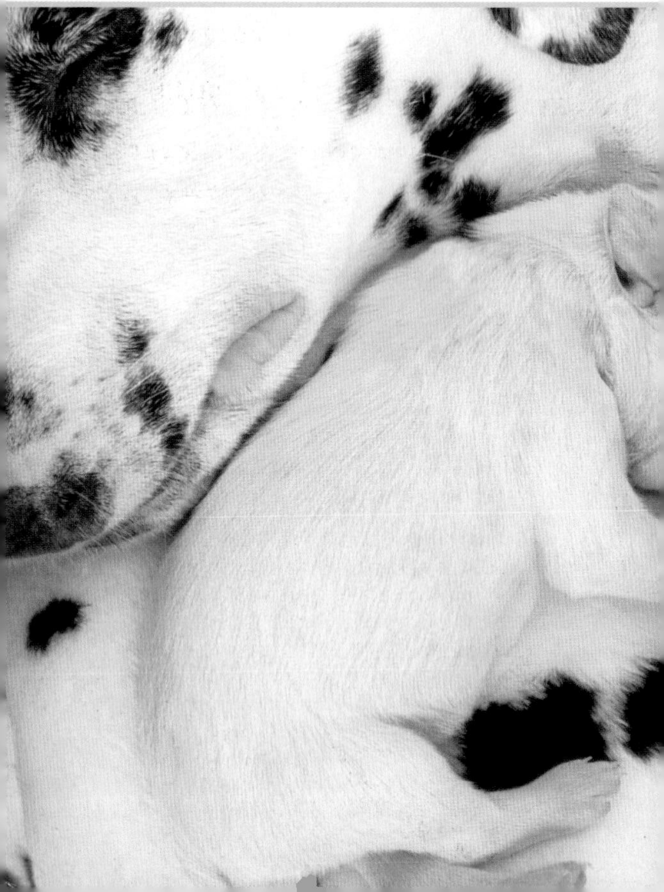

A Dalmatian is born
completely white
and its distinctive spots appear over the next few weeks of its life

LATE BLOOMERS

A newborn Dalmatian looks white because its spots are actually on its skin, hidden underneath the fur. The hair growing from these dark spots turns black or liver in colour over the first few weeks of its life. Some Dalmatians even have spots inside their mouths!

Griffon Bruxellois

The Belgians originally kept the Griffon Bruxellois for hunting rats in stables. Three varieties of this dog exist: two are rough-haired, and one is smooth-haired.

ORIGIN Belgium
HEIGHT 23–28 cm (9–11 in)
COLOUR Black and tan

Wiry coat

Bolognese

A relative of the Bichon Frise, the Bolognese is an intelligent dog that forges a close relationship with its owner.

ORIGIN Italy
HEIGHT 26–31 cm (10–12 in)
COLOUR White

White, non-shedding coat

Dalmatian

The world's only spotted breed, the Dalmatian is a popular family pet. It was once known as the "carriage dog", because it was trained to run beneath or alongside horse-drawn carriages and fire engines.

ORIGIN Unknown
HEIGHT 56–61 cm (22–24 in)
COLOUR White with black or liver spots

Round, well-defined, black spots

Maltese

A devoted, lively, and fun-loving dog, the Maltese is happiest when spending time with its owner. It is intelligent, alert, and a fast learner.

Long, silky, pure-white coat

ORIGIN	Malta
HEIGHT	Up to 25 cm (10 in)
COLOUR	White

Russian Toy

This miniature dog is one of the world's smallest breeds. Despite its fragile appearance, the Russian Toy is very active and energetic. It is rarely seen outside Russia.

ORIGIN	Russia
HEIGHT	20–28 cm (8–11 in)
COLOUR	Fawn; red; black and tan; blue and tan; liver and tan

Short, dense, glossy, white coat

Shih Tzu

The Chinese worshipped this dog as it resembled the Chinese notion of a lion – a holy Buddhist symbol.

This breed is believed to be a cross between the Lhasa Apso and the Pekingese. A good companion dog, the Shih Tzu is favoured by people with allergies because its coat sheds very little.

ORIGIN China

HEIGHT Up to 27 cm (11 in)

COLOUR Variety of colours

Lhasa Apso

Tibetans originally bred the Lhasa Apso to guard temples and monasteries. This small but hardy dog has great stamina and can walk for long distances.

ORIGIN China

HEIGHT Up to 25 cm (10 in)

COLOUR Variety of colours

Pendant ears

Heavy, straight, wheaten and white hair

Pekingese

A loyal companion, the Pekingese was once considered a sacred dog in China and could be owned only by royalty.

Very short muzzle

ORIGIN	China
HEIGHT	15–23 cm (6–9 in)
COLOUR	Variety of colours

Pug

This breed is compact, yet well-proportioned, with a flat, wrinkled face. The Pug is known to have been popular with royalty in Europe.

Smooth, glossy coat

ORIGIN	China
HEIGHT	25–28 cm (10–11 in)
COLOUR	Silver-grey; gold or fawn; black

Japanese Chin

Originally bred to warm the owner's laps and hands, the Japanese Chin does not require much living space.

ORIGIN	Japan
HEIGHT	20–28 cm (8–11 in)
COLOUR	Black and white; red and white

Crossbreeds

Crossbreeds have purebred parents of two different recognized breeds. They are created to mix particular features of their parents. One such example is the Goldendoodle (left) – a mixture of the Golden Retriever and the Poodle. It looks similar to a Poodle, and can serve as a guide or therapy dog like the Golden Retriever.

TREO, THE ARMY DOG
A Spaniel-Labrador cross, Treo served the British Army in Afghanistan by sniffing out bombs. In 2010, he was awarded the Dickin Medal for his bravery.

What is a crossbreed?

A crossbreed is a cross between any two known breeds. Often crossbreeds are specially bred from two purebred animals in order to display special features from each.

Identity crisis

Kennel clubs find it hard to classify crossbreeds because nobody can predict which characteristics of the parents will appear in the puppies. This Goldendoodle is a cross between a Golden Retriever and a Poodle.

Goldendoodle

Happy acciden

The first crossbreeds were accidents. The owners liked the results so much that the selectively bred particula dogs on purpose. One of the first crossbreeds was the Lurcher, a cross between a sight hound and a terrier or herding dog.

Lurcher

unny names

he simplest way to name
crossbreed dog is to
ombine the names of its
arents. So, a Schnauzer
d a Poodle produce
Schnoodle. This
ockerpoo is a cross
etween a Cocker
paniel and a Poodle.

This dog has inherited its
pendant ears from the Spaniel

It has gained its **feathered
coat** from its Poodle parent

ANTI-ALLERGIC

Many people have dog allergies.
Labradoodles (below) are said to
be ideal for allergy-sufferers as
they have non-irritating coats.

Cockerpoo

Crossbreeds

When puppies are produced by parents of two different breeds, they are known as crossbreeds. They generally inherit features from both parents and are given names that reflect their origins.

FOCUS ON...
MIXED BREEDS
Once referred to as mongrels, these dogs have parents of unknown type.

Cockerpoo

Also known as the "Cockapoo", this dog was bred from a Toy or Miniature Poodle and an English or American Cocker Spaniel. It has a wavy coat that sheds very little.

Drop ears

Large, hair-covered paws

ORIGIN	USA
HEIGHT	23–43 cm (8–17 in)
COLOUR	Any colour

Labradinger

This breed is a cross between the Labrador Retriever and the English Springer Spaniel. It is an excellent gundog with the qualities of both its parents. It can be trained both to retrieve like its retriever parent and flush game like a spaniel.

Thick tail

▲ These dogs run, play, and behave just s pedigree dogs do.

▲ No two puppies in a litter with mixed-breed parents look the same.

◀ Most mixed breeds live longer than pedigree dogs. They can live up to 18 years and suffer from fewer inherited diseases.

ORIGIN USA

HEIGHT 46–56 cm (18–22 in)

COLOUR Fawn; liver; chocolate; black

Deep chest

Goldendoodle

This mixture of the Poodle and the Golden Retriever is the newest "designer dog". First bred in the USA in the 1990s, its growing popularity has led breeders to develop it in other parts of the world.

ORIGIN USA

HEIGHT Up to 61 cm (24 in)

COLOUR Any colour

Thick, curly coat

Bichon Yorkie

Double-layered, silky, curly coat

The first Bichon Yorkie was a result of the accidental breeding of a Bichon Frise and a Yorkshire Terrier. It has the liveliness of its terrier parent, combined with the gentle nature of the Bichon Frise.

ORIGIN UK

HEIGHT 23–31 cm (9–12 in)

COLOUR Variety of colours

Bull Boxer

The Bull Boxer dog is a cross between the Staffordshire Bull Terrier and the Boxer. This medium-sized dog is friendly, but can be boisterous, so it needs plenty of exercise.

ORIGIN UK

HEIGHT 41–53 cm (16–21 in)

COLOUR Any colour

Lucas Terrier

Named after its first breeder, Sir Jocelyn Lucas, a British politician and sportsman, this dog is a cross between two terrier types – the Norfolk and the Sealyham.

ORIGIN UK

HEIGHT 23–30 cm (9–12 in)

COLOUR White; light tan

Lurcher

A cross between a sight hound and a terrier, the Lurcher was traditionally used to hunt rabbits and hares. Peaceful and tolerant, it also makes an ideal family companion.

ORIGIN UK

HEIGHT 55–71 cm (22–28 in)

COLOUR Any colour

Fine, pointed muzzle

Long, slender legs

Labradoodle

This breed is a cross between a Labrador Retriever and a Poodle. It is rapidly gaining popularity as a family dog and is on its way to receiving official status in Australia.

ORIGIN Australia

HEIGHT 36–61 cm (14–24 in)

COLOUR Any colour

Tucked-up belly

The Labradoodle was the first
designer dog
to be created

FIRST OF ITS KIND
The Labradoodle first became known in 1988 when an Australian breeder, Wally Conron, crossed a Labrador Retriever with a Poodle to create a guide dog for people allergic to dog fur and dander (flakes of skin shed from a dog's coat). Designer dogs have since become a global trend.

Fascinating facts

PHYSICAL FEATURES

• A dog's whiskers are touch-sensitive hairs, called **vibrissae**, which can detect tiny changes in airflow. They are found on the muzzle as well as above the eyes, and below the jaws.

• Dogs have **three eyelids**. The third eyelid, also known as the "haw", protects the eye and keeps it moist.

• A dog's **shoulder blades** are unattached to the rest of its skeleton. This allows greater flexibility when it runs.

• A dog's **heartbeat** varies depending on its size, and its heart can beat at anything between 70 and 160 times a minute. In comparison, an average adult human's heart beats at around 70 times a minute.

• A domestic dog's **mouth** exerts on average 145 kg (320 lb) of pressure per square inch. Some dogs can even apply up to 200 kg (450 lb) with their jaws.

• The first sense a dog develops is **touch**. Its entire body, including the paws, is covered with sensitive nerve endings.

A dog can be indentified by its nose print, which is as unique as a human fingerprint.

AMAZING ABILITIES

♦ When a dog **howls**, it is believed to be following a primitive instinct to call members of its pack together.

♦ Dogs can be taught to **detect polycarbonate**, a material used in DVDs. Two search dogs with this training found illegal DVDs worth over US$ 3 million.

♦ The motion of throwing a stick arouses the **prey instinct** in dogs – their natural urge to chase down a moving object, as if it is prey.

♦ Dogs have a powerful sense of **hearing**. They are able to hear sounds at four times the distance that the average human can.

♦ At the end of World War I, the German government trained German Shepherds as the **first guide dogs** for war-blinded soldiers.

♦ Therapy dogs are trained to stay **patient, friendly, and calm**. They provide comfort and affection to people who suffer from physical, emotional, or learning problems. Studies show that interacting with dogs lowers stress and helps in relaxation.

OTABLE BREEDS

Boxers may have been named after e way in which they play. At the start of a ame with another dog, a Boxer will stand n its hind legs and "box" at its "opponent".

Chinese legend says that the **how Chow** got its blue-black tongue y licking the blue paint God spilled while ainting the sky.

In Tibet, the **Lhasa Apso** is called the Apso Seng Kye", which literally means 3ark Lion Sentinel Dog". This is because f its lionlike appearance, and its use as a uard dog for Tibetan nobles and holy men.

★ A fisherman's **Newfoundland** is said to have saved the life of French Emperor Napoleon Bonaparte in 1815, when he fell off a ship during his escape from exile.

★ The **Norwegian Lundehund** has six toes on each foot and is able to tilt its head back so it touches its backbone.

★ The **West Highland White Terrier** has an extra strong tail bone. In an emergency (if this dog gets trapped in an underground tunnel), one can pull it out by the tail.

★ The **Golden Retriever** was the first champion breed of the American Kennel Club obedience trials.

OGS IN HISTORY

Pekingese and Japanese Chins ere **highly prized** in ancient China. hey had their own servants and only obles could own them. Stealing them as punishable by death.

Kublai Khan, the great 13th-century ongol leader of China, is said to have wned **5,000 Mastiffs**, the most dogs ver kept by one person.

During the Middle Ages, dogs similar Great Danes and Mastiffs often fought battles, wearing **suits of armour and piked collars**.

▶ Lady, a Pomeranian puppy, was one of three dogs, out of a total 12, to **survive the sinking of the Titanic**.

▶ Smoky, a Yorkshire Terrier owned by an American soldier, Corporal William A Wynne, was a **hero war dog of World War II**. He was credited with 12 combat missions and awarded eight battle stars.

▶ The **only dog to achieve a military promotion** was an adopted stray-Pit Bull mix called Stubby, from the USA. During World War I, Stubby was promoted to sergeant for combat services, which included warning his battalion of surprise chemical gas attacks.

Famous dogs

MYTHS AND LEGENDS

∗ In Greek mythology, **Cerberus, a three-headed hound**, is a fearsome guardian who protects the entrance to the underworld.

∗ **Diana**, the Roman mythological goddess of the hunt, is most often portrayed accompanied by a pack of hunting dogs.

∗ **Anubis**, a dog- or jackal-headed god in Egyptian mythology, is believed to carry the souls of the dead to the after-life.

∗ **Argos** is the faithful dog of the hero Odysseus in the Greek epic *The Odyssey*. According to the story, Argos is the first and only one to recognize his master when Odysseus returns home in disguise after many years away.

∗ **St Guinefort**, a legendary Greyhound from 13th-century France, is recognized by locals as a saint who protects infants. According to legend, Guinefort was killed by his master, who believed that the dog had killed his son. He later realized that the dog had actually protected the child from a wolf.

RECORD BREAKERS

■ The **smallest recorded dog** is Milly, a smooth-haired female Chihuahua, who was measured at 9.6 cm (3.8 in) tall in 2013.

■ The **longest-living** dog was an Australian Cattle Dog called Bluey, who died at 29 years, five months, and seven days.

■ The **highest jump** made by a dog was 172.7 cm (68 in), by Cinderella May, a greyhound from Miami, USA.

■ The **farthest distance crossed** by a lost pet dog to find its way home was 3,218 km (2,000 miles), by Jimpa, a Labrador/Boxer cross.

■ One of the **most expensive** dogs was a Tibetan Mastiff called Hong Dong (Big Splash), who was sold to a Chinese coal baron for 10 million yuan (£945,000).

■ The world's **first cloned dog**, an Afghan Hound named Snuppy, was born at Seoul National University, South Korea, in 2005.

In 1957, Laika, a stray dog from Russia, became the first living being in space and to orbit the Earth.

DOGS IN FILMS

➤ One of the first canine film stars was **Rollie Rover**, a Rough Collie who performed in the silent film *Rescued by Rover*, released in 1905.

➤ The role of **Fang**, the fearsome yet softhearted dog owned by Rubeus Hagrid in the *Harry Potter* movies, is played by a Neapolitan Mastiff.

➤ One of the most famous dog film stars was **Rin Tin Tin**, a German Shepherd who acted in 28 Hollywood silent films. It is said he received over 10,000 fan mails a week.

➤ **Uggie** is a Jack Russell Terrier known for his performance in the films *The Artist*, *Mr. Fix It*, and *Water for Elephants*.

➤ **Nana**, the devoted pet of the Darling family in the book *Peter Pan*, is represented by a Newfoundland. In the story, Nana is a loving and protective caretaker of the children – a typical quality of the breed.

➤ **K9** is a robotic dog from the series *Dr Who*. K9 was originally introduced to make the show interesting for children, but the character was also popular among adults.

➤ The legendary story of **Hachiko**, a Japanese Akita who was known for great dedication and loyalty, was made into the Hollywood film, *Hachi*.

CARTOON DOGS

✦ **Pongo and Perdita** are the famous heroes of a popular animation film by Walt Disney, *101 Dalmatians*. The two Dalmatians rescue their kidnapped puppies from the villain Cruella De Vil.

✦ **Snowy**, the best friend and heroic companion of Tintin from the comic book series *The Adventures of Tintin*, was based on the Wire Fox Terrier breed.

✦ **Snoopy the dog** is a Beagle from the comic strip *Peanuts* created by Charles M Schultz.

✦ **Scooby-Doo**, one of the most beloved of all cartoon characters, is a Great Dane with the robust build and sweet nature that is characteristic of the breed.

✦ **Odie** is the happy-go-lucky Beagle from the *Garfield* comics. He is often depicted as clownish, simple-minded, and an easy victim of Garfield's pranks.

✦ **Pluto**, the devoted pet of Mickey Mouse, is one of the "Sensational Six" – the most famous Walt Disney characters – which includes Donald Duck, Minnie Mouse, and Goofy – another popular Disney dog.

✦ **Spike and Tyke**, the burly Bulldog and his lovable son, are famous characters from the popular animated series *Tom and Jerry*.

Glossary

Almond-shaped eyes Oval eyes with slightly flat corners, found in breeds such as the English Toy Terrier.

Ancestry Lineage, or descent. Dogs have wolf ancestry.

Beard Thick, sometimes coarse and bushy, hair around the lower facial area. Often seen in wire-haired breeds, such as the Kerry Blue and Cesky Terrier.

Belton A coat pattern that is a mix of white and coloured hairs, which gives it a mottled appearance. This pattern is specific to the English Setter.

Black and tan A coat colour with clearly defined areas of black and tan. The black colour is usually found on the body and tan colour on the underparts, muzzle, and sometimes as spots above the eyes. This pattern also occurs in liver and tan, and blue and tan coats.

Blanket Larger areas of colour over the back and sides of the body; commonly used to describe markings in sight and scent hounds.

Breed Domestic dogs that have been bred to have the same distinctive appearance. They conform to a breed standard drawn up by a breed club and approved by an internationally recognized body, such as the UK Kennel Club, the Fédération Cynologique Internationale (FCI), or American Kennel Club.

Breed standard The detailed description of a breed that specifies exactly how the dog should look, the distinct colours and markings, and the range of height and weight measurements.

Brindle A colour mix in which dark hairs form a striped pattern on a lighter background of tan, gold, grey, or brown.

Button ears Semi-erect ears, the top part of which folds down towards the eye, covering the ear opening. They are seen in breeds such as the Pug.

Candle-flame ears Long, narrow, erect ears that are shaped like candle flames. Often seen in breeds such as the English Toy Terrier.

Catlike feet Round, compact feet with the toes grouped together.

Corded A coat type in which curls develop into long cords resembling dreadlocks that cover a dog's entire body. The Komondor and Hungarian Puli have corded coats.

Coursing A sport in which hounds hunt hares or deer by sight.

Docked tail A tail cut to a specific length in accordance with the breed standard. The procedure is normally carried out when puppies are only a few days old. The practice is now illegal (except for some working dogs) in the UK and parts of Europe.

Double coat A coat consisting of a thick, warm underlayer and a weather-resistant top layer.

Dander Tiny flakes of skin from a dog's fur. People with dog allergies are actually allergic to dander.

Drop ears Ears that hang down from their base.

Erect ears Upright or pricked ears with pointed or rounded tips. Candle-flame ears are an extreme type of erect ears.

Feathers Fringes of hair that may be found on the ear margins, belly, back of legs, and the underside of the tail.

Flews A dog's lips. Most commonly used to describe the fleshy, hanging upper lips in dogs of the mastiff type.

Flushing An action by gundogs, which helps hunters by driving out game birds, forcing them to fly into firing range.

Griffon A French word referring to a coarse or wire coat.

Grooming The process of bathing, brushing, and tidying up a dog's appearance.

Group Dog breeds are classified into various groups by the UK Kennel Club, the Fédération Cynologique Internationale (FCI), and the American Kennel Club. These groups are based on the dogs' functions.

Harlequin A colour pattern comprising irregular-sized patches of black and white. The name "Harlequin" only applies to this colour when seen in the Great Dane.

Herding A task that some breeds of working dogs, such as the Border Collie, perform by gathering and driving livestock from one place to another so that they remain together as a group.

Jowls The fleshy part under the lower jaw of a dog. This feature is seen in the Dogue de Bordeaux.

Kennel Club The official body that sets the breed standards. The UK Kennel Club, the Fédération Cynologique Internationale (FCI), and the American Kennel Club are some such bodies.

Mask Dark coloration on a dog's face, usually around the muzzle and eyes.

Matting A tangled or dense mass in a dog's coat.

Molossus A type of large dog in ancient Greece and Rome that is said to have come from a region called Molossia.

Mottling Spots on the coat.

Muzzle Projecting part of a dog's face, usually the nose and jaws.

Pack Usually used to describe a group of sight or scent hounds that hunt together.

Pendant ears A longer and heavier version of drop ears. See *Drop ears.*

Poacher A person who hunts illegally.

Pointing Freezing into position with nose, body, and tail aligned. Some gundogs help hunters to locate prey by "pointing".

Quarry An animal that is pursued by a hunter.

Retrieving Collecting fallen game and bringing it back to a hunter. Retrievers are named for this quality.

Rose ears Small, drop ears that fold outwards and backwards so that a part of the inside is exposed. This type of ear is seen in the Greyhound.

Ruff A long, thick collar of stand-out hair around a dog's neck.

Rump The part of a dog's back nearest to its tail.

Saddle A darker coloured area, not as extensive as a blanket marking, which extends over a dog's back.

Scent trail The track of smell that a scent hound follows to find its prey.

Semi-erect ears Erect ears in which only the tip is inclined forward, as seen in breeds, such as the Rough Collie.

Setting Crouching when picking up a scent. Gundogs "set" to direct the hunter's attention to game, usually pheasant, quail, or grouse.

Sled A vehicle drawn by dogs for transporting people and goods over snow.

Soft mouth Used to describe the tendency of gundogs to carry an object, usually fallen prey, without damaging it. Labrador Retrievers and Spaniels are especially known for having a "soft-mouth".

Speckling Marking with a large number of small spots or patches of colour.

Spoonlike feet Similar to catlike feet, but more oval in shape.

Ticking Small contrasting spots of colour on a dog's coat.

Topcoat Outer coat of hairs.

Tracking The pursuit of prey.

Tricolour A coat of three colours in well-defined patches – usually black, tan, and white.

Tucked up Referring to the belly, a curve in the abdomen towards the hind quarters, commonly seen in breeds such as the Greyhound and the Whippet.

Undercoat The layer of soft hair, usually short, thick, and sometimes woolly, between the topcoat and the skin.

Vermin Small animal pests, such as rodents and foxes.

Weather-resistant Something not affected by weather. Many dogs have a weather-resistant coat, which means that it is water-resistant and protects them from the cold.

Index

Acknowledgments

Dorling Kindersley would like to thank:
Lorrie Mack for supplying portions of the text;
Annabel Blackledge for proofreading; Helen
Peters for indexing; Bharti Bedi, Fleur Star,
Jessica Cawthra, Priyanka Kharbanda, Vatsal
Verma, Vicky Richards, Kingshuk Ghoshal,
and Francesca Baines for editorial assistance;
Chrissy Barnard, Ira Sharma, Kanupriya Lal,
Govind Mittal, and Philip Letsu for design
assistance; Saloni Singh for the jacket; Pawan
Kumar and Balwant Singh for DTP assistance;
Deepak Negi for picture research assistance;
and Gillian Reid for pre-production.

The publisher would like to thank the
following for their kind permission to
reproduce their photographs:

(Key: a-above; b-below/bottom; c-centre;
f-far; l-left; r-right; t-top)

2-3 Getty Images: Moments Frozen in
Time / Flickr (c). 4 Dorling Kindersley:
Natural History Museum, London (b). 6
Dreamstime.com: Moose Henderson (clb);
Smelline (bc); Jamen Percy (crb). 7 Alamy
Images: B Christopher (tr). Dreamstime.com:
Lukas Blazek (bl); Jaymudaliar (c); Christian
Schmalhofer (br). 8 Fotolia: Tatiana Katsai
(l). 9 Alamy Images: Herbert Spichtinger /
Image Source (r). 10 Corbis: Seth Wenig /
Reuters (l). Dreamstime.com: Johannesk (bl).
11 Dreamstime.com: Tandemich (tc). Getty
Images: Datacraft Co Ltd (tr). 12-13 Corbis:
Marek Zakrzewski / Epa (b). 13 Alamy
Images: Klaus–Peter Wolf / Fotosonline (bl).
Dreamstime.com: Nikolay Pozdeev (cr). 14
Dreamstime.com: Anke Van Wyk. 15 Corbis: DLILLC
(tc); Gideon Mendel (br). Dreamstime.com:
Petr Malohlava (tr). 16 Alamy Images:
Juniors Bildarchiv / F369 (br); Richard
Smith / Photofusion Picture Library (cl).
17 Dreamstime.com: Rolf Klebsattel (r).
Getty Images: DEA / G. Dagli Orti (bc).
18-19 Dreamstime.com: Barbara Helgason
(Background). 19 Fotolia: Dogs (tc). 20-21
Getty Images: Corinne Boutin / Flickr. 22
Alamy Images: Dean Hanson / Journal /
Albuquerque Journal / ZUMAPRESS.com.
23 Corbis: Bradley Smith (b). 24 Fotolia:
Nicolas Thibaut / Photononstop (c). 25 Alamy
Images: US Air Force Photo (br). Corbis:
Peter Kneffel / dpa (t). 27 Corbis: Peter
Kneffel / dpa (tr). Getty Images: Philippe
Huguen / AFP (tc); West Coast Surfer (tl).
28-29 Alamy Images: Juniors Bildarchiv /

F274 (crb). 31 Dreamstime.com: Pavel
Shlykov. 32-33 Alamy Images: De
Meester Johan / Arterra Picture Library
(tc). 34 Dreamstime.com: Gea Strucks
(b). 36-37 Corbis: China Photo / Reuters.
41 Dreamstime.com: Glinn (br). 42
Dreamstime.com: Glinn (c). 44-45
Getty Images: Robert Churchill / E+.
47 Dreamstime.com: Glinn (b). 48
Dreamstime.com: Dmitry Kalinovsky.
49 Dreamstime.com: Twildlife (bc). 50-51
SuperStock: Juniors (b). 51 Dreamstime.
com: Vicente Barcelo Varona (tr). Getty
Images: ruthlessphotos.com / Flickr Open
(br). 52 Alamy Images: Ellen McKnight (clb);
Woofl (ccl). 53 Dreamstime.com: Iliyan Kirkov
(b). 54 Alamy Images: Juniors Bildarchiv /
F237 (t). 56-57 Dreamstime.com: Viacheslav
Belyaev (bc). 58 Dreamstime.com: Glinn (b).
59 Dreamstime.com: Yap Kee Chan (br).
60 Korean Jindo: @YeaRimDang Publishing
Co., Ltd. 60-61 Dreamstime.com: Glinn (t).
61 Dreamstime.com: Anna Yakimova (bt).
62-63 Corbis: Zero Creatives / cultura. 64
Alamy Images: Adrian Sherratt. 65 Getty
Images: Samuel Aiken / The Bridgeman
Art Library (bc). 66 Corbis: Bo (bl). 66-67
Dreamstime.com: Henri Faure (bl). 67
Alamy Images: Jerry Shulman (tr). 68-69
Dreamstime.com: Jagodka (bc). 68 Dorling
Kindersley: Cheuk–king Lo / Pearson
Education Asia Ltd (b). 70-71 Dreamstime.
com: Anna Utekhina (tc). 72-73 Corbis:
Steve Bardens. 74-75 Dreamstime.com:
Olga Lukanenkova (t). 77 Alamy Images:
Tierfotoagentur / R. Richter. 78-79
Dorling Kindersley: Rough Guides (bc).
78 Dreamstime.com: Yap Kee Chan (bc).
80 Dorling Kindersley: Rough Guides (c).
82 Alamy Images: Jerry Shulman (br).
84-85 Dorling Kindersley: Rough Guides
(bc). 86 Dreamstime.com: Glinn (c).
86 Dorling Kindersley: Rough Guides (bc).
88-89 SuperStock: Alessandra Sarti / imag /
imagebroker.net. 90 Dorling Kindersley:
Rough Guides (bl). 91 Dorling Kindersley:
Rough Guides (cr). 92 Dreamstime.com:
Rdantoni. 93 Corbis: Heritage Images (b).
94 Alamy Images: Tierfotoagentur / S.
Starick (clb). Dreamstime.com: Anomisek
(cb); Sergey Lavrentev (crb). Getty Images:
American Images Inc / Taxi (cla). 95
Dreamstime.com: Tavphoto (t). Fotolia:
CallalooFred (br). 97 Alamy Images: Juniors
Bildarchiv / F237 (br). 98 Dreamstime.com:
Glinn (cr). 100 Corbis: Vitaliy
Shabalin (br). 101 Dreamstime.com:

Marlonneke (t). 102-103 Dreamstime.com:
Raja Rc (c). 104-105 Dorling Kindersley:
Rough Guides. 105 Dreamstime.com:
Linncurrie (b). 106 Corbis: Dale Spartas. 107
Getty Images: Wichita Eagle / McClatchy–
Tribune (bc). 108 Corbis: Lynda Richardson
(br). Dreamstime.com: Roughcollie (cl).
109 Dreamstime.com: Barna Tanko (t). 110
Corbis: Dale Spartas (bl). Dreamstime.com:
Isselee. Dreamstime.com: Isselee. Getty
Images: Bill Curtsinger / National Geographic
(cl). SuperStock: Justus de Cuveland / im /
imagebroker.net (tl). 111 Dreamstime.com:
Yap Kee Chan (b). 112-113 Dreamstime.
com: Yap Kee Chan (c). 114 Dreamstime.
com: Glinn (bl). 115 Dreamstime.com:
Mohamed Osama (c). 116 Dreamstime.com:
Raja Rc (c). 117 Dreamstime.com: Glinn (cr).
119 Dreamstime.com: Glinn (c). 120-121
SuperStock: Juniors. 122 Dreamstime.com:
Getty Images: Altrendo Images / Stockbyte.
122 Dreamstime.com: Getty Images:
Altrendo Images / Stockbyte. 123 Corbis:
oshihisa Fujita / MottoPet / amanaimages
(bc). 124 Alamy Images: robin palmer.
Dreamstime.com: Barna Tanko (b). 125
Alamy Images: Juniors Bildarchiv RF / F259
(bc); Juniors Bildarchiv RF / F145 (br).
Dreamstime.com: Yap Kee Chan (b);
Roughcollie (c). 126 Dreamstime.com:
Dreamstime.com: Glinn (c). 129
Dreamstime.com: Lee6713 (t). 130-131
Getty Images: Kathleen Campbell / Stone.
132 Dreamstime.com: Okssi68 (cl). 132-133
Corbis: Akira Uchiyama / Amanaimages
(bc). 133 Dorling Kindersley: Cheuk–king
Lo / Pearson Education Asia Ltd (c). 136
SuperStock: Juniors. 137 Getty
Images: AFP (bc). 138 Alamy Images:
Michael Gamble. Fotolia: Carola Schubbel
(cr). 139 Fotolia: Caleb Foster (t). Getty
Images: LWA / Digital Vision (bl). 140-141
Dorling Kindersley: Rough Guides (bc).
141 Getty Images: Hillary Kladke / Flickr
Open (tr). 143 Alamy Images: John Joannides
(b). 144-145 Dreamstime.com: Gordhorne.

All other images © Dorling Kindersley

For further information see:
www.dkimages.com